Railway Memories

ARDSLEY
WAKEFIELD
&
NORMANTON

STEPHEN CHAPMAN & PETER ROSE

BELLCODE BOOKS
10 RIDGE BANK TODMORDEN
LANCASHIRE OL14 7BA

The most out-
standing fea-
ture of the old
W a k e f i e l d
Westgate sta-
tion was its 97ft
clocktower. This
is how it looked
fromthe station
forecourt on 4th
August, 1965.
(British Rail)

Copyright 1994   Bellcode Books

ISBN 1 871233 05 4

Edited by Stephen Chapman.

Associate Editor: Peter Rose.

Printed by The Amadeus Press Ltd.,
Huddersfield.

FRONT COVER: Class A2 4-6-2 No. 60533 *Happy Knight* **rolls into Wakefield Westgate with
the 9.55 am Leeds - Doncaster on 7th September, 1962.**
**FRONTICEPIECE: It may not have been another Crewe as the Victorians expected, but
Normanton was certainly more important than it is today. On 27th June, 1962 Carlisle
Kingmoor Black Five 4-6-0 No. 45018 was pausing there with a northbound express.**
**BACK COVER(TOP): The pride of the line through Wakefield Westgate is still the Yorkshire
Pullman. This is it 1961-style, being whisked through Ardsley station by A1 Pacific No. 60135**
Madge Wildfire **on 4th November.**
**BACK COVER(BOTTOM): Normanton-based Stanier Class 3 2-6-2T No. 40179 calls at
Wakefield Kirkgate with a Normanton-Sowerby Bridge local on 30th August, 1961. (***All Peter
Rose)*

INTRODUCTION

Not so many years ago you could stand anywhere in the countryside around Wakefield and never be more than two or three miles from railways of widely different characters.

On one side there could be a main line carrying glamorous expresses hauled by the most famous locomotives in the land; on the other, a bumpy, weed-covered mineral track along which a determined little colliery engine would be dragging a line of unwilling coal trucks.

Heavy haul freight trains would be trundling night and day in and out of important marshalling yards as meandering stopping passenger services bound together the mining communities which won the coal the railways carried.

Today, as InterCity 225 trains glide in and out of Wakefield Westgate and only railbuses call at the remnants of Kirkgate and Normanton stations, this all seems so long ago.

Railway Memories No. 6 takes us back to the time when the wastelands of Ardsley bustled with railway activity, when top link expresses served three main line stations, when Wakefield and Normanton were bastions of steam, and when Healey Mills was the centre of the West Riding freight universe.

This volume extends to the outskirts of Leeds so as to meet up with Railway Memories No. 3 and features some of the

CONTENTS

colliery railways which kept steam alive in this part of the country well into the 1970s.

Below: Now waste ground alongside the two tracks of the electrified Leeds-Doncaster main line, Ardsley was, until the mid-1960s, a bustling railway centre with marshalling yards and a mjaor locomotive depot. Here, J6 0-6-0 No. 64182 comes off the Tingley line with the 12.30 pm(Saturday) from Bradford City Road. (David Holmes)

SETTING THE SCENE

AS with so many places in the North, the complex railway system covered by this book owes its beginnings to George Hudson, the Railway King.

His aim, above all else, was to not only develop a through main line from Leeds and York to London Euston, but to protect it from all potential competition.

Hudson's two companies, the North Midland from Leeds to Derby, and the York and North Midland linking it to York met just a mile north of Normanton, at Altofts Junction.

When these lines opened in July, 1840, they set in motion developments which would establish Normanton as a railway junction of such importance that many Victorians expected it would rival Crewe.

Completion of the Manchester and Leeds Railway from across the Pennines via Hebden Bridge the following year reinforced their expectations.

Plugging Wakefield into the railway network, it joined the North Midland at Goose Hill Junction, just south of Normanton station. From there the M&L enjoyed running powers over the NMR into Leeds.

Even at this early stage, the basis of a main line system was in place with Normanton at its centre.

Methley Junction was established on 27th July, 1840 when the YNMR's mile-long spur from Whitwood Junction, Castleford, was completed. This enabled trains to run direct from York to the NMR's Hunslet Lane station in Leeds.

Right from the start, this village which came to have three stations, was to play a critical role in the bitter inter-company rivalries of the day.

The Whitwood-Methley spur was the key component in Hudson's controversial insistance that York-Leeds trains should run via the NMR to Hunslet Lane, milking traffic away from the older Leeds & Selby Railway.

A few years later, Methley Junction was the scene of a confrontation between two companies which almost ended in tragedy.

Despite the start of the Railway Mania, no further lines were opened in these parts for several years, but the local busines community was pressing for improved links between the increasingly industrial West Riding and the Humber ports.

As a result, the Wakefield, Pontefract and Goole Railway was formed, opening the direct line between those three places on 1st April, 1848. It was followed on 1st October, 1849 by another line running direct from Methley Junction to Pontefract, both of which were vested in the Lancashire and Yorkshire Railway, newly constituted from the Manchester and Leeds in 1847.

Much to Hudson's horror, they were destined to give the Great Northern Railway direct access to the West Riding for its new services from London Kings Cross.

Using the L&Y's route through Askern and Knottingley, the GNR was able to run right into Wakefield Kirkgate, while the Pontefract-Methley line allowed it to reach Leeds over the North Midland line.

As a result, Hudson and the Midland Railway, which by this time had superseeded the NMR, demanded a promise from the GNR that it would never attempt to build its own line into Leeds.

Failing agreement, the Midland said that GN trains would be stopped at Methley Junction until passengers had coughed up a toll to Midland officials.

On the evening before the line's proposed opening on 4th September, 1849, GN officials, suspicious that the Midland was up to something, sent a light engine from Doncaster to Methley where the crew found that the points had been removed from the junction, action which might well have derailed the first GN train.

Events some years later which brought the railway to Ardsley and spawned Wakefield Westgate station avoided any further Methley confl;icts.

On 3rd October, 1857 the Bradford, Wakefield and Leeds Railway opened a line from Ings Junction, on the L&Y just west of Wakefield Kirkgate, to Ardsley, Beeston and Leeds, giving GN trains a direct route from Wakefield to Leeds. The same year also saw completion of the Leeds , Bradford and Halifax Junction

The Lancashire and Yorkshire main line from Manchester met the Midland from Derby to Leeds at Goose Hill Junction, Normanton.
While his train was being held on the Midland Down Goods line, Leeds Holbeck fireman Roy Wood climbed the tender of his Black Five 4-6-0 to take this picture of Crab 2-6-0 No. 42790 powering a semi-fitted freight along the Up Main. The L&Y lines are on the left.

line from Ardsley via Tingley to Bradford, enabling the GN's trains to reach that city in December.

Meanwhile, another of Wakefield's principal and surviving routes had opened. The Rotherham, Barnsley, Wakefield, Hull and Goole Railway from Sheffield was completed in January, 1850 and joined the L&Y by a Wakefield-facing junction at Horbury.

The next major piece of railway, from Wrenthorpe Junction, just north of Westgate, to Batley via Ossett was opened by the BW&L in stages between 1862 and 1864. Before it was fully opened, the BW&L changed its name to the West Yorkshire Railway which was in turn swallowed up along with the direct Wakefield-Leeds line by the expanding GNR in 1865

The countryside around Wakefield was changing noticably in the mid 19th century with bigger coal mines appearing among the rolling fields. As the industry grew, its owners stepped up pressure for better links with their customers and the Humber ports.

One result was that the GN, Midland and North Eastern railways joined forces to build the 6-mile Methley Joint Railway from Lofthouse Junction (Methley) to Lofthouse North Junction where it joined the Wakefield-Ardsley line. On the way it served Newmarket

Silkstone Colliery at Stanley. Goods traffic commenced in June, 1865 and Leeds-Ardsley-Pontefract/Castleford passenger trains in 1869.

On 1st February, 1866 the West Riding and Grimsby - another joint venture, this time involving the GN and the Manchester, Sheffield and Lincolnshire companies - was opened between Wakefield and Doncaster. This provided the GN with its most direct and fastest Leeds/Bradford-London route - the route used today - and gave, through running powers agreed in 1892, the MS&L(shortly to become the Great Central) access to Leeds and Bradfordfor its expresses from such places as Sheffield and Cleethorpes.

The opening of a spur by the L&Y from its Wakefield-Pontefract line to the Midland line at Oakenshaw South in 1861 and by the WR&G from Sandal to the Midland line at West Riding junction in 1868 allowed Midland trains from the south into both Westgate and Kirkgate stations.

A direct route from Wakefield to Dewsbury was opened up by the GNR in 1874 with completion of a 2.5-mile line from Runtlings Lane Junction, near Ossett on the Wrenthorpe-Batley line.

The Batley line was downgraded as a result, carrying only local goods and passenger trains while the Dewsbury line became one of three routes by which portions of Kings Cross expresses travelled to and from Bradford.

The coal owners were still unhappy with the service provided by the existing railway companies and actively encouraged new, independant lines.

One of these, designed to link the Barnsley coalfield with Hull and Goole was the Barnsley Coal Railway which was only completed, after 20 years of wrangling, with the backing of the MSLR.

It ran from Barnsley to the Leeds-Doncaster line at Nostell, the final section from Applehaig, south of Royston, being opened in August, 1882. A triangular junction at Nostell enabled MSLR trains to run direct to the company's own port at Immingham.

A month later it began carrying a Barnsley Court House-Leeds Central passenger service.

The Midland Railway made a small addition to its network in 1885 when it opened a branch from Snydale Junction, just south of Normanton, to the Don Pedro and Featherstone Main collieries.

The following year, the L&Y opened a 1.25-mile connection from Crofton West to the WR&G at Hare Park which, among other things, allowed GN Kings Cross-Halifax expresses to reach Kirkgate direct, eliminating a reversal down the 1 in 100 incline from Westgate.

Beeston Junction, a railway landmark once heralding the approach to Leeds, was founded in 1890 when the GNR completed a line from Batley via Tingley. With this came a circular Leeds Central-Wrenthorpe-Dewsbury-Tingley-Leeds passenger service. A second circular service introduced in 1893 when other lines were opened was one run jointly by the GN and L&Y between Leeds, Tingley, Batley, Cleckheaton, Low Moor, Pudsey and Leeds. Beeston Junction was also traversed by Bradford-Tingley-Leeds and L&Y Barnsley-Leeds services.

Developments such as these still did nothing to satisfy the coal owners and during the 1880s the Charlesworth family, with pits around Rothwell and Stanley, sought a connection with the newly-opened Hull and Barnsley Railway.

The H&B's failure to secure running powers into northern parts of the West Riding led to the promotion of two independant lines. One was the East and West Yorkshire Union Railway from Ardsley to the H&B at Drax.

The scheme was thwarted by a lack of

The railway first came to Ossett courtesy of the Bradford, Wakefield and Leeds when it opened the Wrenthorpe-Batley line. In 1874 the GNR opened up a new line to Dewsbury and Ossett was put on a through Wakefield-Bradford route which came to be used by Bradford portions of London expresses.

In this 1962 view a Fairburn 2-6-4T and B1 4-6-0 No. 61110 pull a Bradford-Scarborough excursion out of the station and towards Wakefield. Ossett still had a large goods yard at that time and the goods shed is on the left. *(Roger Hepworth)*

The East and West Yorkshire Union Railway was a fascinating independant system built to carry minerals from several pits, coking works and quarries. Its operating centre was at Robin Hood where there was also a passenger station which saw regular services for only a few months in 1904. Passing through with a Stourton to Ardsley goods on 15th March, 19611 was J6 0-6-0 No. 64226. *(Peter Cookson)*

capital so the Charlesworths picked up the pieces and supported a strictly local line linking the GNR at Lofthouse North with their collieries and quarries around Robin Hood and Rothwell.

Thus was born a celebrated railway which remained wholly independant until becoming part of the LNER under the 1923 grouping.

Its steeply graded line opened in May, 1891, being worked by the GNR between Lofthouse and Robin Hood and by Charlesworths' own locomotives over the remainder. It became a through route in April, 1895 when the South Leeds Junction Railway connected Rothwell to the Midland Railway at Stourton.

Three months later the EWYU began operating the whole of its route itself, and the South Leeds Junction Railway in July, 1896.

In 1898 the EWYU opened a branch from Robin Hood down a 1 in 86 gradient to Patrick Green under only the second Light Railway Order to be granted in accordance with the 1896 Light Railways Act. From there a mineral line continued down a 1 in 44/45 incline to Newmarket Colliery.

A LRO was granted in 1901 allowing all the EWYU to be operated as a light railway. From January, 1904 the company tried to run a Leeds Wellington-Robin Hood passenger service, worked on its behalf by the Midland Railway, while it used its own locos and coaches for a service to Patrick Green.

The Robin Hood-Leeds service lasted only a few months but Robin Hood and Rothwell stations remained intact, used by occasional excursions, until the 1960s.

Beeston Junction was expanded in 1898 by the opening of the GNR's goods branch to Hunslet East while on 4th March, 1905 the L&Y completed Wakefield's last new line - 8.25 miles from Crofton West to Shafton Junction where it met the Dearne Valley Railway which the L&Y agreed to operate. With it came a spur from Crofton South to East, enabling trains from the DV to run in the Goole direction.

The DV and its Crofton connection carried coal from the many pits it served but in 1912 the L&Y introduced a steam railmotor passenger service between Wakefield Kirkgate and Edlington Halt, near Doncaster.

The main line network was complete but a second system had steadily been superimposed upon it. This was a host of colliery lines which interconnected the various mines with each other and with their associated coke, chemical and brick works as well as carrying coal from collieries to main lines.

Some were waggonways used to take coal from early pits to river wharves since before the first main line railways were built. Some colliery railways remained in use until the virtual anhialation of Britain's coal mining industry began in the late 1970s.

Notable colliery railways, under the control of the National Coal Board since 1947, included those linking Lofthouse and Normanton St. John's collieries with staithes at Stanley Ferry, where the Aire and Calder Navigation 'New Cut' crosses the River Calder, the line between St. John's and Park Hill pits, as well as lengthy connections with the main lines such as those from Crigglestone to Denby Grange and Emroyd collieries.

The 1.5-mile St. John's-Stanley Ferry line carried compartment boats - known as 'Tom Puddings' - between the pithead where they were loaded with about 40 tons of coal and Newland Basin. There they were lowered down an inclined track into the water so that a tug could haul a line of them, train fashion, to Goole where their contents were tipped into waiting colliers.

Mining and production complexes hugged the main lines, the biggest being at Lofthouse and in the Altofts and Whitwood area which was home to the West Riding and Whitwood collieries, each with their own extensive internal rail systems.

Even in the 1970s one of the NCB's Leeds-built Hudswell Clarke 0-6-0Ts or Hunslet 0-6-0STs could still be seen at Newmarket or Methley Savile while blasting its way over dubious track with a train of familiar side tippler wagons.

Back on the main line system, the two most important station to begin with were Normanton and Wakefield Kirkgate, Normanton especially so, being at the crossroads of main lines to London, Leeds, York and Manchester.

Temporary facilities were soon replaced by a permanent station with extensive Italianate Villa style buildings, completed in 1841 and run by a joint committee of the companies which used the station. An hotel and refreshment rooms connected to the station by a covered footbridge were added shortly after.

By the 1850s, the station had been extended to include two island platforms while marshalling yards were subsequently added on the west side and a locomotive depot betwen the station and Altofts Junction.

Unfortunately, Normanton's hopes of becoming another Crewe were soon dashed as the opening of other routes diverted traffic away.

In what must have been one of the earliest rationalisation schemes, the statio n was reduced to a single island platform(with bays inlet at each end) in 1871 although, at nearly a quarter of a mile, it was the fourth longest in the country.

The Settle and Carlisle line brought something of a revival when Normanton became a refreshment stop for Anglo-Scottish expresses but this lasted only until the Midland Railway introduced refreshment cars in 1895. From then on Normanton settled into the role of a principal secondary rail centre until the 1960s when further rapid decline set in. In 1994 only the island platform remained, the buildings replaced by waiting shelters and a shrubbery. Even Goose Hill Junction has been obliterated.

By the 1850s, Wakefield Kirkgate was gaining importance, again due to the growing influence of the GNR whose Kings Cross trains terminated there after running via Doncaster and Knottingley.

The GN had its own platform but in 1853 it agreed with the L&Y to build a fine new station.

Complete with imposing buildings and an overall trainshed roof, it was ready for use by 1857 and remained a joint station, finally LMS/LNER until nationalisation in 1948.

Adding to Kirkgate's importance were other companies which acquired running powers there, such as the NER with a service between Hull and Halifax, (though not Hell!) and from 1866, the London and North Western whose workings included the Holyhead-York cattle trains which continued until the 1960s.

But even Kirkgate began to decline once most GN expresses were routed direct into Westgate over the WR&G.

Westgate station was opened on its present site in 1867 following completion of the WR&G, its most prominent feature being a 97ft clocktower.

The station was accompanied by a large goods warehouse and a three-road engine shed.

One of Wakefield"s premier expresses was the Leeds/Bradford - Kings Cross West Riding, seen here under the charge of A1 Pacific No. 60114 *W.P. Allen* while getting away from a permanent way slack at Sandal in 1957. On the left is the embankment carrying the abandoned connection to the Midland main line at West Riding Junction. *(Tony Ross)*

It was rebuilt in 1966/7 when the buildings and clocktower were swept aside by a contempory brick and glass structure.

In its heyday the Wakefield area was at the crossroads of three main trunk routes radiating to the four corners of Britain.

The most prestigous of these was and still is the Leeds-Doncaster main line through Westgate, forming as it does an important tributary of the East Coast main line.

Since the days of the GNR the fastest West Riding-London trains have sped through Ardsley and called at Wakefield. They included The West Riding Limited, The White Rose and The Yorkshire Pullman(still running in 1994).

Until 1967 when the practice was switched to Leeds City, through carriages were attached and detached at Westgate, being hustled between there and Bradford by the classic Gresley N1 0-6-2Ts and later by ex-LMS 2-6-4Ts or B1 4-6-0s.

The Midland through Normanton carried equally important expresses to a greater variety of destinations.

Along with the St. Pancras-Glasgow Thames-Clyde Express and its Edinburgh counterpart the Thames-Forth(later The Waverley), were trains linking West Yorkshire with the Midlands and the West Country like the Bradford to Paignton Devonian.

The most important train on the third major route, the L&Y main line, was the celebrated 10.30 am Liverpool Exchange to Newcastle dining car express. This route also carried principal trains between Liverpool, York, Goole and Hull, besides express newspaper trains carrying northern editions from the Manchester presses.

There was once a continental boat train from Liverpool which divided into three portions at Kirkgate - one to York, one to Hull Riverside Quay where it connected with NER/LNER sailings to Zeebrugge, and one to Doncaster where it was attached to a York-Harwich boat train.

Local services were many and varied and included Leeds-Ardsley-Methley-Castleford/Pontefract; Leeds-Sheffield Victoria; Leeds-Doncaster via Westgate and Kirkgate; Bradford - Dewsbury -

9

Coal to the west and empties coming back east were the lifeblood of the L&Y Calder Valley line, once one of the most intensively-worked stretches of railway outside London. Wakefield-based WD 2-8-0 No. 90326 trundles a load of coal along the busy four-track section through Horbury Millfield Road at 2.11 pm on 18th February, 1961. *(David Holmes)*

Ossett-Wakefield; Leeds-Methley-Knottingley; Leeds City-Cudworth-Sheffield; Normanton-York; Normanton-Sowerby Bridge-Manchester Victoria; Wakefield Kirkgate - Goole - Hull; Kirkgate-Barnsley Exchange; and Kirkgate-Cleckheaton-Bradford.

What fun we could have had with a West Yorkshire Metro Day Rover ticket if all these and the circular services through Beeston Junction were still running today!

As coal became more and more the driving force behind the railways, so new facilities had to be created and existing ones expanded to handle the increasing volumes of freight generated by something like two dozen pits in an area ten miles by ten.

The yards at Ardsley and the large locomotive depot were developed late in the 19th century not only for handling coal but as a reception and forwarding point for all GN freight to and from West Yorkshire. Principal trains were formed or broken up there while trips radiated to depots throughout the Leeds, Bradford and Wakefield areas. Extensive sidings

were also developed at Wrenthorpe Junction while the Midland had yards at Normanton as well as Stourton and Carlton (Cudworth).

On the L&Y system, Crofton Hall sidings, situated just south of Crofton South on the Dearne Valley Junction line handled huge tonnages of coal, an expanded Wakefield L&Y loco depot providing the power.

Catering for coal saw creation in the early 20th Century of a new major railway location as sidings were laid out on a green field site at Healey Mills.

Between the late 19th Century and the mid-1920s, the Midland main line south of Snydale Junction and the L&Y from Wakefield to Brighouse were quadrupled to accommodate the coal trains.

With all this freight activity, a number of firms were established to build and repair wagons, the best known being Charles Roberts who set up a wagon works in Wakefield in 1865, later moving to the site of Horbury iron works where it still operates alongside the Canadian Bombardier-Prorail group.

There have been many changes to the

railways around Wakefield and Normanton over the years, not least the massive contraction brought on by the Beeching era and the unbelieveable disappearance of coal mining.

Some passenger services were lost or reduced as early as the late 19th Century but that was mainly to accommodate new developments. Others succumbed in the early 20th Century to more convenient electric trams, one casualty being the Chickenly Coddy which ran along the downgraded Batley line between Ossett and Chickenly Heath until 1909.

It was after the second world war, however, that the system really began to contract.

The Beeston Junction to Batley line closed to passengers in 1951 and to all through traffic in 1953. The Dearne Valley passenger service, never well patronised, was also axed in 1951, while in 1957 it was the turn of the Ardsley-Bradford stopping service, withdrawn on 25th February.

The 1960s were the decade of mass closures which had such a devastating effect in the West Riding. The East and West Yorkshire Union was the first to go, the Robin Hood-Stourton section being severed by works for the abortive Stour-ton marshalling yard in June, 1961. The branch to Newmarket Colliery was shut on 9th March, 1963, the colliery then being served solely by its triangular connection to the Methley Joint. Closure of the entire Lofthouse-Stourton line in October, 1966 meant the end of this interesting system.

The introduction of diesel multiple units to several local services in 1957/8 was a great success on some routes - such as the newly-introduced Leeds-Wakefield Kirkgate-Barnsley-Sheffield service - but they failed to save many others from the axe.

The Wakefield-Dewsbury-Bradford local service went on 7th September, 1964 taking Ossett station with it. The Methley Joint passenger service ceased on 2nd November, Ardsley station closing at the same time.

The Dewsbury line closed completely in 1965 while the Methley-Stanley section of the Methley Joint continued to serve Newmarket Colliery until the late 1970s.

Also, by 1965 only the Nostell-Wharncliffe Woodmoor portion of the Barnsley Coal Railway remained, devoid of booked trains - and all had gone by 1969.

The Ardsley-Bradford line was finally

Diesel mutliplt units were introduced to many West Riding services in the 1950s but they failed to stave off the Beeching axe. A pair of two-car Metro-Cammell units leave Ossett while on a Bradford to Wakefield service in summer, 1962. *(Roger Hepworth)*

hit in 1966 when the Bradford portions of Kings Cross trains were rerouted via the Wortley curve in Leeds. Only a stub from Ardsley to Tingley gas works and Morley Top survived until about 1970.

Also in 1966, new connections from the Midland main line near Cudworth to the Dearne Valley allowed huge chunks of the DV to be closed along with the line from Crofton.

The Wakefield-Pontefract line closed to passenger traffic in January, 1967, sacrificed, it was said, to accommodate intensive services of Merry-Go-Round block coal trains running between the Barnsley area and the new power stations at Eggborough and Ferrybridge. The former GNR goods branch to Hunslet East closed in the same year, abolishing Beeston Junction.

Passenger services were withdrawn from the Methley-Cutsyke line from October, 1968 when Leeds-Knottingley trains were rerouted via Castleford Central, a move involving reinstatement of the Methley-Whitwood curve, abandoned some years before.

That year saw even more significant changes. Not only were Leeds-Cudworth-Sheffield stopping trains withdrawn on 1st January, but Leeds-St. Pancras/West of England expresses were taken off the Midland line and routed via Wakefield Westgate, using the Swinton and Knottingley line from Moorthorpe to reach Sheffield.

South of Normanton, the Midland line remained busy with freight until May, 1973 when the prospect of severe mining subsidence on the S&K forced not only the Leeds expresses back on to it but also those from the York direction which started running via Normanton. Many Leeds trains still served Westgate, however, gaining the Midland via Kirkgate and Oakenshaw South.

The situation was again reversed in the early, 1980s when Leeds expresses reverted to the Moorthorpe route while some, including those from York, ran via Doncaster.

After that, the only passenger trains to regularly use the Midland main line were the summer Saturday 07.39 Leicester to Scarborough, and the Friday 22.39 Bradford-Paignton which was also the final passenger service over the Oakenshaw-Oakenshaw South curve.

They were switched to other routes after the 1986 summer timetable and within two years through freight was also withdrawn south of Goose Hill. The

The Leeds City-Cudworth-Sheffield stopping service became a closure victim on 1st January, 1968. Stanier Class 3 2-6-2T No. 40082 passes the West Riding Silkstone Colliery as it approaches Altofts and Whitwood with the 5.23 pm from Leeds on 20th June, 1959.
The Altofts-Methley section of the North Midland line became freight only in 1990 when Altofts station closed and its remaining couple of passenger trains were diverted via Castleford. (Neville. Stead)

Although very much reduced, Healey Mills yard was still handling large amounts of traffic in the late 1980s.
Class 37 No. 37244 sets out with the afternoon Network Coal train to Mossend on 9th September, 1988. The diesel depot is behind the central lighting tower and the administrative block on the right. *(Stephen Chapman)*

once 4-track main line was downgraded until all that remained in 1994 was a double track from Crofton East to Cudworth for use by a daily sand train.

A major blow on 5th January, 1970 was the axeing of York-Manchester Victoria trains which had linked Normanton and Wakefield Kirkgate with the opposite side of the Pennines for 130 years. Horbury and Ossett station closed at the same time while the once important Kirkgate station was left as little more than a Paytrain halt.

The Methley-Altofts section lost most of its passenger trains in summer, 1988 when all but a handful of Leeds-Barnsley-Sheffield trains were rerouted via Castleford.

The rundown of freight mirrored the collapse of the coal industry, all colliery railways and main line connections having disappeared by or during the 1980s.

Acres of sidings that once forwarded thousands of tons of coal a week became wasteland and superstores while the vast Healey Mills marshalling yard was scaled down. Even the 1,000-ton MGR trains that plied constantly between pits and power stations disappeared.

Just about the only coal trains left in 1994 were passing through on their way across the Pennines to the Fidlers Ferry power station, Warrington, and the only originating coal from Wintersett opencast near Nostell. The St. John's complex was swallowed up by the huge Welbeck landfill project for which a new rail terminal stands on the site of Locke's Siding to receive spoil in MGR trains from the Selby mine.

The only general freight depot left in 1994, handling mostly steel and other bulk goods, was the Cobra Railfreight terminal next to Kirkgate station.

The news is not all bad though and decline has been tempered with a few positive developments, thanks mainly to the support of local authorities through the West Yorkshire Passenger Transport Executive.

Remaining passenger services were saved and improved, and some closed stations reopened. Fitzwilliam, closed in 1967, was the first when it reopened as an unstaffed halt in March, 1982. Similar stations followed at Sandal and Agbrigg in November, 1987 and at Outwood in 1989.

May, 1992 saw passenger trains reinstated over the Wakefield-Pontefract line, bringing a mini-revival to Kirkgate station which became a focal point for local services to Sheffield, Castleford, Leeds, Knottingley and Manchester.

Today, Wakefield Westgate stands on one of the country's most successful InterCity main lines - electrified in 1989 as part of the East Coast main line project.

But by the time this volume of Railway Memories is published, work should have started on building the Port Wakefield international freight terminal, which will be served direct by trains to and from the Continent via the Channel Tunnel, giving some hope for the future.

POLISH & PARAFFIN

Harold Wainwright, who retired in 1993 as principal of British Rail's operations training centre at Webb House, Crewe, began his railway career at Wakefield Kirkgate in 1954:

As a youngster in the late 1940s, he often visited Wrenthorpe West box where his relief signalman cousin sometimes worked,

"Like all signal boxes then, it had an atmosphere of smoke, steam, oil, metal polish and paraffin. Other characteristics were the tall desks with high stools; wooden armchair held together with signal wire and padded with well-worn cushions; polished lino floors, burnished lever tops, bright golden brasswork, coal fires, chemical loos, flag sets, oil lamps and strings of detonators. Although the traffic was varied freight/passenger, there wasn't a lot of it even in those days.

"My cousin's younger brother became a signalman at Roundwood Colliery, situated in a deep cutting with the colliery sidings at a much higher level; so much so that the colliery engine could only manage about six wagons at a time between the pit and the exchange sidings."

After joining the railway, Mr. Wainwright underwent the training and exams necessary to be a signalman before being given his first, temporary posting at Locke's Sidings.

"I will never forget my first shift alone. The responsibility was awesome but with over 90 moves a shift one didn't have time to worry.

"Open continuously 3am Monday to 6am Sunday, the box was situated between the L&Y lines facing the colliery sidings and the Midland lines which ran immediately behind. Normanton was a notorious bottleneck and the Down Midland Goods line could be occupied for hours by freight trains whose crews were regularly relieved in the loop.

"Locke's controlled the Up and Down Main and Down Goods with connections to the colliery sidings on the Down side.

"Lockes and Park Hill collieries were the same pit but the empties went in at Lockes and the fulls came out at Park Hill. Two trains of up to 65 empty wagons from Healey Mills were dealt with each weekday, one mid-afternoon and the other at 3 am. Trains stopped clear of the crossover and the engine ran round via Goose Hill. Other traffic permitting, train crews preferred to shunt from the Up Main across all lines to facilitate the reading of hand signals on the curve. Even then, the signalman would often use his higher vantage point to relay signals from guard to enginemen. When the empty sidings were full, long rafts of wagons were propelled towards the colliery round a sharp left hand curve. I often wondered what would have happened if the colliery loco came down at the same time.

"Traffic passing Lockes included Trans-Pennine expresses, three coach locals and all kinds of freight. The rising gradient was quite steep on the Down and the sight and sound of a B16 lifting a Healey Mills to Teesside freight away from a check at the home signal was not to be forgotten."

In late summer, 1954, Mr. Wainwright moved on to Crofton South - 112 levers and quite a culture shock.

"The whole area seemed to be on an embankment, the box facing the junction between the Up Sorting and Departure sidings, the Down Empty sidings being to the left. Up the hill was Crofton Hall which controlled departures from the Empty side to the Dearne Valley collieries and loaded trains on to the Up Arrival lines. To the right down the hill was Crofton West. Immediately in front of South box was the right hand junction to Crofton East and Crofton Tip.

"Traffic was almost exclusively coal. Sorting was by gravity shunting which could be unpredictable due to a combination of inefficient wagon brakes and human failure. As a result, coal dust got everywhere. The sidings formed deep valleys of rails through mountains of coal spillage. The signal box was dirty too and there was little incentive to clean it up - even if you had the time.

"Fully permissive working applied to all lines in all directions, maximum 6 trains in section. A count was kept on the red clock face L&Y block indicators. There were around 100 movements per shift, late turn being the busiest with terminating trips on the Up and light engines to Wakefield shed.

"My stay at Crofton was mercifully short and I transferred to Wakefield Kirkgate Centre box on 13th December, 1954.

"It was different again with no night or Sunday shift. Its sole purpose was to control movements within the train shed.

"The four lines through the station comprised Up and Down Platform and Up and Down Through lines. Double crossovers(scissors) were provided in both Up and Down lines with extra crossovers between the through lines. Outer home signals with calling-on arms were provided outside the station with the main signals slotted with Wakefield East and West boxes respectively. The constaraints posed by the trainshed roof meant that Inner Home signals inside the station were of the disc(dolly) type.

"LMR Station Yard Permissive working was employed, allowing full permissive working with passenger trains, light engines, and engines with brake vans. Freight trains were not accepted behind passenger trains, however. Wrong direction working was authorised in both directions and was used for passenger engine changes on the Up or for propelling stock in from Wakefield Exchange sidings.

"There were more movements in the Down

Harold Wainwright began his signalling career at Locke's Siding where the L&Y main line serviced St. John's Colliery.
WD 2-8-0 No. 90610 approaches Locke's Siding with a 1960s unfitted express goods from the Wakefield direction. The signal box closed on 28th February, 1982 following resignalling in the area. *(Peter Cookson)*

direction because all trains had to pass through the station, whereas on the Up there were extra lines outside the trainshed controlled directly by East and West boxes. There were 120/130 moves per shift with several passenger peaks, the busiest being 6 to 7pm with several engine changes"

Aspiring to become a station master, Mr. Wainwright moved into the clerical grades and joined the district operating superintendant's office at Westgate. Following a station master's course and successful application for such a posting he moved away from the area in January, 1957.

He returned in early 1963, seconded to a NE Region team set up to train staff and help commission the big new marshalling yards. Healey Mills Down yard was commissioned first, followed by the Up yard two or three months later. This complete, he left to become station master at Sowerby Bridge in June, 1964.

"I returned to Healey Mills as asistant yard master in January, 1965. At the time the AYMs, one on each shift, had a roving brief throughout the yard.

"One night in February, 1965 after a heavy snowfall, I went to investigate a reported smell of gas at the Horbury end of the Down Departures. The engineers had been installing propane point heaters and as I arrived a steam-hauled goods was leaving with hot coals dropping from its firebox. The next thing was a huge explosion which knocked me flat. The whole area as engulfed in flame but it soon subsided and I was unhurt apart from being shocked. Rats were blamed for eating the plastic propane pipes.

"The following summer a train arrived on the Down Receptions with a wagon on fire, a Hybar full of straw. We cut it out of the train and took it to the end of the Down Staging lines where the water column made short work of it. But while climbing into the wagon to direct the bag I overbalanced and fell into two feet of dirty water, grabbing the red hot hybar on the way in and burning my fingers.

"Summer and autumn, 1966 was, I think, the busiest time that Healey Mills ever saw. It was not unusual to arrive for late turn to find the yard and receptions virtually full with trains queued almost back to Mirfield.

"The yard's defined role was to collect traffic into economical train loads and act as a supply point for empties, only we always seemed to be receiving more traffic than could be disposed of. Thus we had to make special moves to clear priority loads and keep collieries supplied with empties.

"Our shift was the first to move a complete train of Type 3 diesel, 50 empties and brake van off the Down Main via a reception line, over the hump and through an empty siding in the Up yard where it was re-manned and sent to the Barnsley branch. This line-clearing short cut was done several times after.

"We also took the all-time record for the most wagons humped in one 8-hour turn - 1,596 wagons. We did it because on the day there was a lot of coal traffic which was easy to hump in rafts of five wagons. We had two continuous pilots which were radio controlled with drivers relieved for meal breaks. It was not many years later that yards were lucky to achieve such a figure in a day, let alone a shift.

On 16th July, 1955, when J6 0-6-0 No. 64277 was heading the 3.42pm Leeds Central to Doncaster, Beeston Junction was in a tranquil country setting.
Today, the suburbs of Leeds have swallowed up the fields.
The Hunslet East branch goes off behind the train and the splitting home signals, left arm off for the main line, denote the junction Tingley.
(David Holmes)

ARDSLEY & THE GREAT NORTHERN

Owing to its involvement in the West Riding and Grimsby Joint south of Wakefield, the Great Central Railway had a considerable presence in the area and its influence survived almost to the end of steam.
Robinson GC Class C13 4-4-2T No. 67438 leaves Beeston Junction behind while working the 4.16pm Leeds Central to Castleford on 23rd May, 1956. The southbound spur of the Tingley flyover is starting to climb away on the right. *(David Holmes)*

Above: Pacific likeA3 No. 60047 *Donovan* were normal super-power for the 4.47pm Leeds Central to Doncaster local, seen storming the 1 in 99 climb from Beeston Junction to Ardsley Tunnel on 24th June, 1961. The train is just passing beneath an impressive flyover which carried the Leeds-bound track of the Tingley line as part of an elaborate flying junction. *(David Holmes)*

Below: On a crisp 4th November, 1961, V2 2-6-2 No. 60908 rushes the 10.15am Leeds to Doncaster towards the viaduct which carried both tracks of the Tingley branch over the main line.

SHORT MEMORIES

25.2.57: Wakefield-Dewsbury-Bradford services go over to DMU operation, some running through to Goole and Hull from March, 1958.

September, 1957: 350hp diesel shunter D3381 delivered new to Normanton.

September, 1957: Four B1 4-6-0s transferred to Wakefield regularly work to Rose Grove with the 12.30am Goole to Blackburn goods.

16.9.57: Methley North station closes.

21.9.57: J50 0-6-0Ts 68895/8/937 transferred to Ardsley.

October, 1957: N1 0-6-2T 69474 is transferred to Ardsley

A bright autumn morning and the Tingley line viaduct provides a perfect setting for Class A4 Pacific No. 60006 *Sir Ralph Wedgewood*, as it nears Ardsley Tunnel with the 9.45 am Leeds Central to Kings Cross on 4th November, 1961
(Peter Rose)

On 26th October, 1959, the 6.12pm Kings Cross to Leeds express collided with a light engine just north of Ardsley station.

The inspecting officer investigating the accident, Colonel McMullen, concluded that it was caused by a lack of clear instructions governing the method of signalling light engines needing to enter a block section while shunting from Down to Up main lines.

The signalman at Ardsley Station box forgot that an engine was standing in the path of the express on the Down Main awaiting its movement to the Up. Also. the engine's driver failed to remind the signalman of his position, believing that the shunt signal he was standing at was track circuited and would display his position automatically.

Colonel McMullen's report gives an insight into the method of working at Ardsley at the time: "The Ardsley-Bradford line leaves the main Doncaster-Leeds line at the north end of the station and the Up Bradford line includes a slip connection with the Down Leeds to form a Down/Up crossover.

"Because of the proximity of the signal boxes on the Leeds route, Ardsley Station cabin has no advanced starting signal on that line ahead of the junction and the platform starter, a 3-aspect searchlight signal (with junction indi-

tor for the Bradford line), governs entry into the block section to Ardsley North box. This signal also acts as Ardsley North's distant. At the time of the accident there were no block controls on Ardsley Station Down starting signal, nor was there a track circuit to indicate an engine standing clear of the crossover."

On the evening concerned, the engine moving from the yard on the Down side and destined for the engine shed on the Up side was sent forward on the Down line to stand clear of the crossover before shunting to the Up.

The Down starting signal was cleared to a yellow aspect for this movement by the Ardsley Station signalman although he had not offered the engine to Ardsley North and had it accepted.

The Ardsley Station signalman could not immediately allow the engine on to the Up line, as he had given precedence to an Up Bradford train. As this train cleared the junction, the express was offered by Ardsley South and the Ardsley Station signalman in turn offered it to Ardsley North, forgetting about the light engine.

Fortunately, the Ardsley Station signalman did not clear his Down distant signal for the express and its speed was, as a result, reduced to about 35mph and casualties were light.

Top: A1 Pacific No. 60135 *Madge Wildfire* is still fighting the 1 in 99 grade as it emerges from Ardsley Tunnel with the 3.32 pm Leed-Kings Cross on 21st August, 1961. The 4-coach Bradford portion will be added at Wakefield, making a total of 12 coaches.

Centre: Approaching Ardsley with the Up Yard on the right, A4 No. 60008 *Dwight D. Eisenhower* heads one of the Leeds-Doncaster line's premier trains, the London-bound White Rose, on 25th October, 1961. *(Both Peter Rose)*

Bottom: J50 0-6-0T No. 68915 completes the 1 in 73/109 climb from Beeston Junction and is entering Tingley on a Bradford-bound transfer freight in 1957. The line from Ardsley approaches from the right background while on the left is the start of sidings serving Tingley's hilltop gas works *(Tony Ross)*

Above: With Ardsley West signal box on the right, J39 0-6-0 No. 64820 slogs up the Tingley line with a train of mineral wagons on 4th November, 1961. *(Peter Rose)*

Below: Class A1 4-6-2 No. 60118 *Archibald Sturrock* approaches Ardsley from the Leeds direction with the Up Harrogate Sunday Pullman in May, 1958.
The line on the left is a goods loop off the Tingley branch and left of that are the Tingley branch sidings. The Tingley main lines are further left behind the bank. *(Tony Ross)*

Above: As Ardsley's J39 0-6-0 No. 64820 starts toiling its way up the line towards Tingley, beyond Ardsley West signal box, on 4th November, 1961, a WD 2-8-0 rumbles gingerly towards Ardsley, even though the distant signal for Ardsley Station is in the 'off' position. Below: A splendid view of Ardsley North yard on 4th November, 1961. Another Ardsley J39, No. 64705, comes off the Tingley line as Hunslet-built 204hp 0-6-0 diesel shunter No. D2608 pushes a rake of wagons into the loading dock, one carrying one of the containers so familiar at the time. *(Both Peter Rose)*

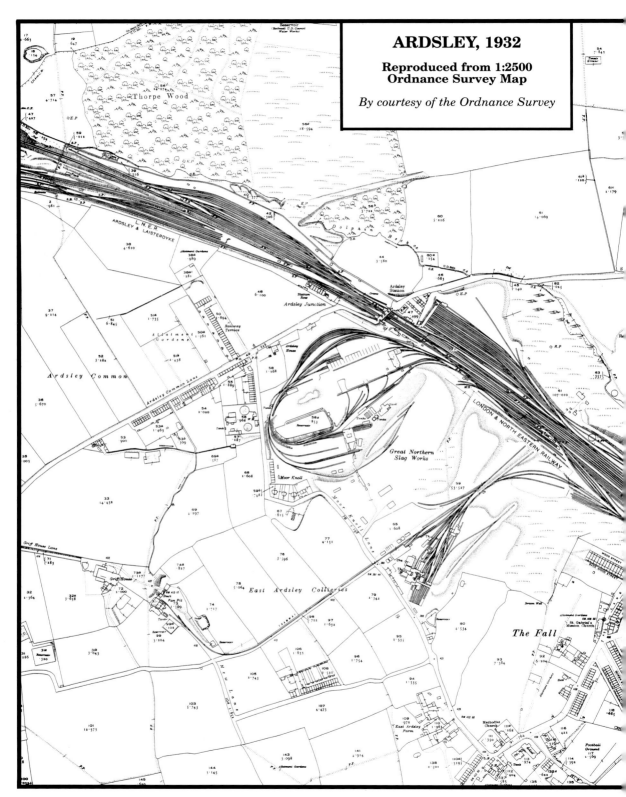

ARDSLEY, 1932

Reproduced from 1:2500
Ordnance Survey Map

By courtesy of the Ordnance Survey

Thorpe on the Hill

Robin Hood Quarries

Brick Works

Dolphin Lane

Allotment Gardens

Spring Wood

Sewage Works

Bowling

Spring Lane Sidings

Sewage Works

Lingwell Nook

White Hart

Anton Green

Lingwell Gate

23

Above: Standing by the goods yard crane on 31st March, 1962 while on shunting duties was No. 67777, one of the half-dozen L1 2-6-4Ts then allocated to Ardsley. The trackless loading dock and the stump of the crane, on the Up side, were just about the only reminders of the Ardsley railway centre still to be seen in 1994. *(Roy Wood)*

The way in which lamp oil was delivered by train to Ardsley was an example of the simple ingenuity which in those days kept the railways moving.
Full oil drums came from Leeds Central carrying a brass plate which read: "Sig. Eng. to Ardsley."
Once the drum was emptied, the single screw holding the plate on would be undone and the plate reversed, revealing the instruction: "Ardsley to Sig. Eng." which would ensure the drum's safe delivery back to Leeds. If only life were that simple today!

Below: The signalman watches as B1 No. 61310 draws up alongside Ardsley Station box on the same day. The goods loading dock is on the left *(Roy Wood)*

Ardsley station, five platforms but rather basic facilities was set amid a sea of sidings holding large numbers of wagons, most of them for coal.

Bottom: Passengers on the narrow island platform welcome Fairburn 2-6-4T No. 42073 with the Saturday Only 1.52pm Castleford-Leeds Central on 5th November, 1960. The Old Coal yard is in the left background and the Down yard on the right . *(David Holmes)*

On weekdays in summer, 1957 Ardsley was served by 33 trains to Leeds Central, 20 to Castleford via Stanley, and 10 to Doncaster. The 9.40pm Bradford-Kings Cross called there at 10.7.

The station closed when Methley Joint passenger trains were withdrawn on 31st October, 1964.

Top: Calling there on the last day, complete with tail lamp, was the 10.12am Leeds-Pontefract DMU.

Centre: The gloom of Ardsley's last day was deepened by fog, as seen from the Wakefield end. *(Both Brian Myland)*

Above: Another view of Ardsley station in rather better weather as A2/3 Pacific No. 60523 *Sun Castle* rushes through with a Kings Cross to Leeds express on 31st March, 1962. *(Roy Wood)*

Below: This view, of Ardsley J6 0-6-0 No. 64277 trundling a short train along one of the Up goods lines was taken from the footpath which led from Fall Bridge to the station. In 1994, all except the two fast lines had gone and the site of Ardsley station and yards trembled day and night to the roar of the M1 motorway. *(Peter Rose)*

DEPARTURES FROM ARDSLEY YARDS JUNE,1965

DOWN YARD

09.15	SX	8P31	to Tingley gas works.
10.45	ThO	8K07	Askern to Tingley gas works.
13.15	SX	8P25	to Hunslet East.

SPRING LANE

03.00	MX	7N09	19.55 Kings Cross-Leeds Wellington Street.
03.35		5P32	to Bradford Adolphus Street.
04.00		5P35	to Halifax.
04.20		7P26	to Hunslet East
04.30	MO	6N20	to Leeds Wellington Street.
05.05		7P17	to Bradford Adolphus Street.
06.05	SX	8P41	to Stanningley.
06.55		7P30	to Hunslet East.
07.00		8P26	to Tingley gas works.
07.30	SX	8P29	to Armley Moor.
08.20		8K12	to Laisterdyke.
08.40		8P23	to Hunslet East.
08.45		8P22	to Laisterdyke.
09.05	SX	7P27	to Hunslet East.
09.40	SO	8P26	to Tingley gas works.
10.10	SX	8P53	to Leeds Wellington Street.
11.30	SX	8P31	to Laisterdyke.
11.35		8P23	to Hunslet East.
13.05	SX	8P19	to Bradford City Road.
13.40	SX	8P21	to Tingley gas works.
16.00	SX	8P21	to Bradford Planetrees.
16.05	FO	8P25	to Hunslet East.
16.20	FSX	8P25	to Hunslet East.
19.45	SX	8P25	to Hunslet East.
20.05	SX	7P54	to Leeds Wellington Street.

UP YARD

09.15	SX	7P26	Empties to Roundwood Colliery.
11.45	SX	7P06	Empties to Castle Hills.
14.10	SX	7E85	to North Lincoln Jn.
15.45	SX	7P02	to East & West Yorkshire Sidings.
21.30	SX	4E50	to Whitemoor.
22.15	SX	5M13	to Mottram.
22.35	SX	6E57	to Ferme Park.
22.55	SX	7M77	to Ickles.
23.15	FO	7E53	to Doncaster Bank.
23.30	FSX	7E53	to Doncaster Bank.

OLD COAL YARD

00.50	MX	7H23	23.30 Bradford Adolphus St. - Hull.
02.25	MX	8P33	to York.
04.15	MX	8E10	to Ickles.
04.45	MX	6P10	to Doncaster Bank.
05.00	MO	8K10	to Dewsbury.
05.15	MX	8K62	to Healey Mills.
05.40	SX	8J75	to Waterloo Coll. Sdgs.
05.40	SO	8M27	to Mottram.
06.30	SX	8M27	to Mottram.
07.30*	SX	8P02	to Stourton.
08.00	SX	8E81	to Scunthorpe.
09.00	SX	8K15	to Turners Lane Sdgs.
09.05	SO	8K15	to Turners Lane Sdgs.
09.45	SX	8J75	to Waterloo Coll. Sdgs.
17.05	SO	8K20	to Healey Mills.
20.05	SO	5E58	to Doncaster Bank.
20.20	SO	8P33	to York(suspended).
20.35	SO	8M47	to Ickles.
21.10	SX	4E56	20.05 Leeds Wellington Street - Kings Cross.
21.30	SX	4E50	to Whitemoor.
22.15	SX	5M13	to Mottram.
22.35	SX	6E57	to Ferme Park.
22.55	SX	7M77	to Ickles.
2315	FO	7E53	to Doncaster Bank.
23.30	FSX	7E53	to Doncaster Bank.

From Spring Lane.

SHORT MEMORIES

Above: Looking south underneath Fall bridge as Ardsley's own O4/7 2-8-0 No. 63857 leaves Spring Lane yard with a coal train on 27th January, 1962. The fast lines pass to the left of Ardsley South signal box while the motive power depot is to the far left. The O4 is one of those rebuilt from 1939 with a shortened GNR-type O2 boiler but retaining its original GC smokebox.

Below: The steps down from the bridge to the footpath gave young sptters a grandstand view of operations. A group of youngsters watch excitedly as Britannia Pacific No. 70008 *Black Prince* pulls an empty wagon train out of the yards on the same day. *(Both Brian Myland)*

13.5.60: Special trains run from Wakefield Kirkgate to London for the Wakefield Trinity v. Hull Rugby League cup final. Hauled by Holbeck Class 5s, most of the 11-coach trains are assisted up the steep Oakenshaw spur to the Midland main line by Wakefield B1s which are detached at West Riding Junction.

18.6.60: BR class 4 2-6-0 76022 of Kirkby Stephen shed works a Normanton-Oldham goods.

21 & 22.6.60: Sheffield Millhouses Class 2 2-6-0 46494 passes Horbury & Ossett with the 8.44am Halifax-St. Pancras.

24 & 30.6.60: Millhouses BR Class 2 2-6-0 No. 78024 is on the Halifax-St. Pancras express.

Ardsley motive power depot was opened by the GNR in 1892, mainly to cater for growing coal traffic.

As a result, its allocation was mostly goods engines, although it did have some passenger types, especially in later years when some Pacifics were based there.

Coded 37A after nationalisation, it was top shed in the Eastern Region's West Yorkshire district. In 1956, Eastern and London Midland sheds in West Yorkshire were transferred to the North Eastern Region and Ardsley became 56B in the Wakefield district.

Ardsley closed in October, 1965 and within two years the site was cleared.

Right: Inside the shed with numerous J50 0-6-0Ts in May, 1954 was Copley Hill A1 Pacific No. 60134 *Foxhunter*. (*J.C. Hillmer*)

LOCOMOTIVES ALLOCATED TO ARDSLEY

Summer 1950

B1 4-6-0: 61029 *Chamois*/ 61031 *Reedbuck*//61033 *Dibatag*/85/96/1297/1309/10; B4/4 4-6-0: 61482 *Immingham*; Q4 0-8-0: 63202/4/5/17/21/3/5/6/7/34/6/40/3; J3 0-6-0: 64116/9/29/42; J6 0-6-0: 64174/82/208/14/67/72/7; J39 0-6-0: 64749/51/4/60/96/9/801/6/11/25/36/9/40/72/96 /907 /11/ 79/85; C12 4-4-2T: 67386; C14 4-4-2T: 67440/1/3/4/5/6/51; J52 0-6-0ST: 68790/848/71/2; J50 0-6-0T: 68896/900/1/3/4/7/9/10/4//5/6/9/21/30/1/8/9/47/8/9/51/66; N1 0-6-2T: 69452/61. Total: 88.

Autumn, 1962

A3 4-6-2: 60036 *Colombo* /60069 *Sceptre*/ 60070 *Gladiateur* / 60077 *The White Knight*/ 60080 *Dick Turpin*/60092 *Fairway*; A1 4-6-2: 60123 *H.A.Ivatt*/60131 *Osprey*/60134 *Foxhunter* / 60135 *Madge Wildfire*; B1 4-6-0: 61013 *Topi* / 110/1295/7/1310; K3 2-6-0: 61853/ 6/ 917/34/80/4; O4 2-8-0: 63584/605/33/724/823/57/64/85; J39 0-6-0: 64719/49 /54/6/60/96/818 /40/ 79/911/8/69; L1 2-6-4T: 67742/55/63/5/6/77; J94 0-6-0ST: 68008/11/5/45/9/62; J50 0-6-0T: 68934/5/7/65; WD 2-8-0: 90100/26/230/6/40/361/405/9/65/81/625/42/4; Hunslet 204hp 0-6-0 diesel: D2586/ 95/6/7/603/4/5/6/7/8/17. Total: steam 70, diesel 11.

Below: Is this you? Young visitors to the running shed on 4th July, 1964 pose in front of V2 2-6-2 No. 60923. WD 2-8-0s and a Fairburn 2-6-4T are on either side.

Above: Inside the original GN repair shop with its timber roof beams, the same youngsters on the same day with B1 4-6-0 61013 *Topi* . (Both Arthur Chesters)

The GN coaling stage at Ardsley was replaced by a modern mechanical plant in the early 1950s.

Top: Well polished J50 No. 68922 attends the old coaling stage which still gave an impression of being active. on 3rd January, 1960. *(Brian Myland)*

Centre: With the new plant behind, another pristine engine, Britannia Pacific No. 70053 *Moray Firth* comes off shed in the late 1950s. *(C. Marsh)*

Bottom: The old Great Central maintained a considerable presence at Ardsley and GC locos were based there for freight and passenger work.

The Robinson C14 4-4-2Ts were a classic example, such as No. 7443, pictured on 6th September, 1947.

Behind the loco is the old manual ramped coaling stage and its huge water tank. A pair of GN 6-wheeled coaches stand alongside. *(G.H. Butland)*.

Top: Ardsley engine-men: driver B. Myers and fireman on the footplate of C14 4-4-2T, LNER No. 7443, on 6th September , 1947. *(G.H. Butland)*

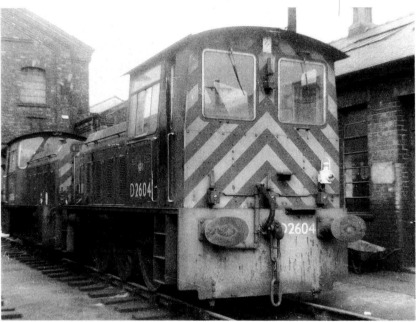

Centre: More recent times with Hunslet 204 hp 0-6-0 diesel shunters Nos. D2604 and D2606 outside the repair shop on 26th September, 1961. These locos were used for shunting the yards. *(Adrian J. Booth)*

Bottom: The ex-GC 4-6-0s were favourites among the Ardsley fleet and the last survivor of the Immingham class, *Immingham* itself, was shedded there.

LNER B6 No. 1348 was nearing the end of its days when photographed on 6th September, 1947. *(G.H.Butland)*

Engines on Ardsley:
Above: The Great Central influence was still evident well into BR days. Here, Class O4/7 63570 comes off shed on 21st August, 1961. *(Peter Rose)*

Below: The Gresley Class N1 0-6-2Ts were stalwarts of ex-GNR local passenger services in West Yorkshire. In this May, 1954 view, Nos. 69484 and 69463 are on shed with an ex-GC 2-8-0. *(J.C. Hillmer)*

Jim Lodge's work in the Outdoor Machinery dept. often took him to Ardsley shed, of which he recalls: "It had a good repair shop with overhead cranes driven by an endless hemp rope - quite an antique.

" The shop was between the shed and the various workshops which themselves had a more than usual number of machine tools, machinery you'd expect for an 'A' shed.

"Like other LNER sheds, Ardsley always smelled different to the ex-LMS sheds - dismal, dank and gassy with a greenish haze which was probably due to the coal they used.

"Like any big shed Ardsley had its share of humour, like the apprentice who couldn't leave things alone.

"An electrician told him: 'Don't touch that it's only tied up with string.'

"The inquisitive youth couldn't help himself and the sand hopper came crashing down."

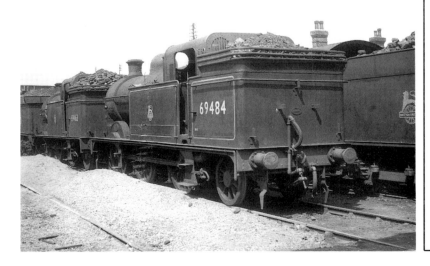

Engines on Ardsley:
Above: The once ubiquitous J6 0-6-0s of the old GNR were in BR days usually covered in grime from their generally mundane labours, but LNER No. 4182 looked much more presentable when photographed outside the original shed on 6th September, 1947. *(G.H.Butland)*
Below: In more usual condition at 3pm on 5th December, 1960 were Ardsley stalwarts, J50/2 0-6-0T No. 68900 and J6 No. 64222. No. 68900 was one of the original 18 rebuilt by the GNR in 1922 from the smaller J51. The shed is visible under the bridge. *(David Holmes)*

Above: Lofthouse Colliery, between Ardsley and Wakefield , was a huge complex with coke ovens, a brickworks, the Yorkshire Alum Works and rows of sidings lined with wagons. This is how it looked on 4th November, 1961 when A4 Pacific No. 60006 *Sir Ralph Wedgewood* was passing with the 10am Leeds to Kings Cross..

Below: In less than three years the scene at Lofthouse Colliery has changed considerably. The signalling has been rationalised and the Down sidings are little used and overgrown. Steam still has a place, however, as Copley Hill B1 No. 61031 *Reedbuck* rolls past with the 10.48am Leeds Central to Cleethorpes on 4th August, 1964. Just visible on the right is a colliery saddle tank.. *(Both David Holmes)*

Above: B1 No. 61320 rattles the numerous windows in the unusual Lofthouse and Outwood GN side buildings while racing a Leeds portion of the 4.8pm from Kings Cross through the station in the evening of 24th May, 1960. Behind the Up platform is the curve to the Methley Joint line. The station closed completely on 13th June but today a new one, just called Outwood, stands nearby.

Below: By summer 1957 the only regular passenger train using the Methley Joint platforms, was the 6.30am Wakefield Westgate-Castleford Central. However, the South-East curve was still used by summer Saturday trains such as the 10.52am Castleford Central to Cleethorpes, being hauled towards Wakefield through the disused platforms on 4th August, 1964 by Stanier 2-6-4T No. 42650 and B1 No. 61388. The houses of Railway Terrace, empty and boarded up, were just about the only trace of this scene left in 1994. *(Both David Holmes)*

Above: On 4th August, 1964 steam passenger trains traversed all sides of the Lofthouse triangle in the space of an hour. The others are on pages 35 and 36. This was the 11..58 Bradford-Bridlington, rounding the North-East curve onto the Methley Joint behind Ivatt 2-6-0 43141 and B1 61110. *(David Holmes)*
Right: One mile 600 yards further on was Stanley station, seen from the level crossing on 31st October, 1964, its last day before closure. *(Geoff Lewthwaite)*

STANLEY 1907
Not to scale

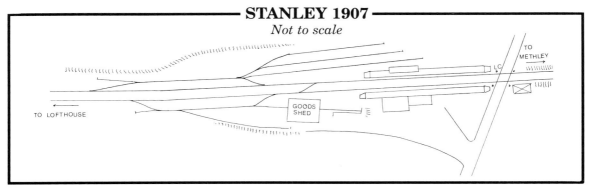

TO METHLEY

LC

GOODS SHED

TO LOFTHOUSE

Six years after the end of BR steam and nearly 10 years after the Methley Joint closed to passengers, steam could still be found shunting coal wagons at Newmarket Colliery.
Above: On 16th July, 1974, NCB Hudswell Clarke 0-6-0T No. S103(1864/52) places wagons in the trianlge of sidings connecting the colliery to the Methley Joint line. (Adrian Booth)

SHORT MEMORIES

Summer, 1960: The 8.44am Halifax - St. Pancras and return trains are two of the few regular passenger workings over the Horbury-Crigglestone curve. Booked power to/from Sheffield is a Low Moor 2-6-4T but on 28th June, the duty was entrusted to Walton (Liverpool) 4F 0-6-0 No. 44188.

2.7.60: Glasgow Corkerhill Jubilee No. 45687 *Neptune* passes Normanton with the southbound Devonian.

Summer, 1960: Three of Ardsley's four K3 2-6-0s loaned to Low Moor for services to the Lancashire coast.

April, 1961: Drewry 204 hp diesel D2323 allocated new to

Right: Taking water outside the engine shed on 14th June, 1972 was Austerity 0-6-0ST *Jess*, built by the Hunslet Engine Co. in 1943.
Regular steam operation ended at Newmarket in 1974 when the Hudswell Clarke diesels took over. But S103 went back to work during 1976 while the diesels were under repair.
The internal rail system remained in use by diesels taking spoil to a tip near Bottom Boat until lorries took over in late 1981. The colliery closed in 1983 after 150 years' operation.
David Holmes.

In summer, 1957 the Methley Joint was served by 21 weekday trains each way, although there were no Sunday trains. Not all trains stopped at Methley South. There were also the Saturday Only 8.59am Bradford-Bridlington, and 2.20pm return, which called at Stanley and Ardsley until 7th September. The line speed was 40mph and it had signal boxes at Lofthouse East, Stanley, Charlesworth's (Newmarket Colliery), Methley South, and Lofthouse Jn. (Methley).

Top: The line's last booked steam passenger train, the 1.49pm Saturday Castleford-Leeds, rolls into Methley South behind 2-6-4T No. 42094 on 23rd September, 1961. *(David Holmes)*

Right: Closure is just a week away as a member of staff poses by Methley South's ornate buildings on 27th February, 1960. *(G.C. Lewthwaite)*

Joining British Railways on the East and West Yorkshire Union at Rothwell, David Holmes eventually became a local station master.

"The EWYU was a by-way even in 1954. The only engine types I ever saw there were J6 0-6-0s, J52 and J94 0-6-0STs.

"The only passenger trains were an odd enthusiasts' special and Mrs. Cotton's excursions. Mrs. Cotton was the wife of the EWYU station master and still organised seaside outings even though they had moved to Stanningley.

"One of my first jobs was to write out hundreds of invoices for the movement of coke from Robin Hood coking plant as well as coal from Newmarket and other local collieries.

"I spent two years at Hunslet East where a colossal amount of freight was handled. At 4.30 am a trip came from Ardsley bringing fruit and veg from Wisbech and Covent Garden.

"In the late 1960s, when station master at Castleford I had charge of the Methley Joint which by then went just to Newmarket colliery,

"In 1968 the method of working was by train staff and ticket as it was impossible to maintain any electrical methods due to constant theft of wire. It also meant that a BR man had to be employed at Newmarket and I used to go there to pay his wages. 'One Engine in Steam' would have been cheaper but there was always the prospect of two trains needing to be on the branch at once, due to the amount of traffic and the line's limited opening hours resulting from Methley South and Lofthouse Junction boxes only being open one shift.

"Most of the Newmarket coal went to Skelton Grange power station, near Leeds on the Midland line, so trains had to reverse at Glasshougton, Castleford.

Above: The triangular junction at Wrenthorpe was where the branch through Ossett to Dewsbury left the Leeds-Doncaster main line, while there were extensive sidings inside the triangle, just two of which survived, disused, in 1994.

Sweeping round past Wrenthorpe North Junction with a Sunday Leeds to Kings Cross express in May, 1958 was A1 Pacific 60125 *Scottish Union*. *(Tony Ross)*

Below: Ossett station at 8am on 11th May, 1963. B1s 61189 *Sir William Gray* and 61240 *Harry Hinchcliffe* prepare to leave with a London-bound special for the Rugby League cup final between Wakefield Trinity and Wigan as porter Wicks wheels a barrow across the island platform. *(Roger Hepworth)*

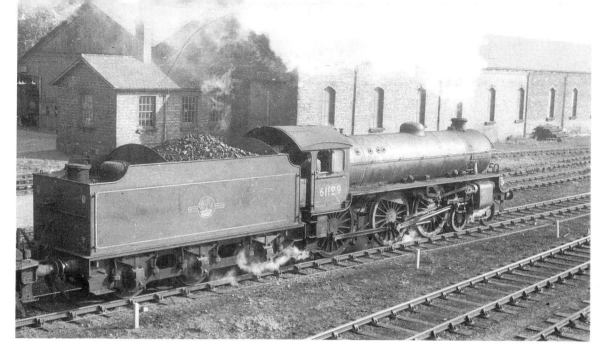

More views of Osset station in the 1960s:

Above: The Rugby League cup final special setting off with the station's large goods depot in the background.

Centre: A Sunday Bradford-Cleethorpes excursion arrives from the Dewsbury direction in 1961 headed by the incongruous combination of J6 0-6-0 64208 and Black Five 4-6-0 45208. (*Both Roger Hepworth*)

Below: The quite extensive Ossett layout as it was in 1933. (*Not to scale*)

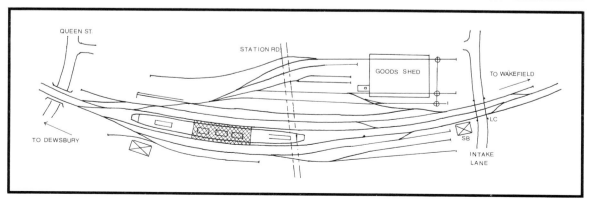

Above: The Dewsbury loop left the Batley line at Runtlings Lane Junction.
With the Batley line diverging to the right, J39 No. 64801 approaches the junction with Bradford to Kings Cross through coaches in 1954. *(Tony Ross)*
Right: One of Ardsley's Hunslet diesels passes Ossett on its way to shunt Dewsbury Railway Street goods depot in autumn, 1963.*(Roger Hepworth)*

FLUSHDYKE 1908

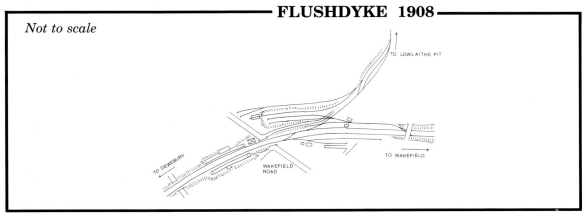

Not to scale

TO LOWLAITHS PIT

TO DEWSBURY

WAKEFIELD ROAD

TO WAKEFIELD

Above: With the former GN/GC/MR joint goods yard on its right, J6 No. 64226 arrives at Wakefield Westgate with a trip freight from Ardsley on 3rd June, 1961. In the background, above the open wagons, is the site of the 3-road engine shed. The goods yard finished up as a distribution terminal for new cars brought in by block trainload and such traffic forms part of this train's consist, but by the early 1990s even that had gone. In the distance, beyond the back of the train, is Balne Lane signal box. *(Peter Rose)*

BALNE LANE: In shunting or transferring vehicles to or from the main line and Westgate goods yard or carriage sidings at Balne Lane, there must at all times be a brake van at the south end and a man in charge of the brake. Vehicles which are being shunted must not be left on the main line at or near Balne Lane Junction. *Eastern Region(North) Sectional Appendix, 1968*

Below: Leaky A3 Pacific No. 60063 *Isinglass* passes Westgate North signal box on its way out of the station with the 7.45am Kings Cross to Leeds on 3rd June, 1961, having left the Bradford portion in the platform. *(Peter Rose)*

Wakefield Westgate yard and goods warehouse looking west on 27th July, 1949 with the site of the engine shed on its top right flank. The shed had been demolished by this time and the roads used for stabling coaches, although the turntable was still present. Towards the top of the picture can be seen Wrenthorpe Junction and the Dewsbury branch going away left, together with the expanse of Wrenthorpe yard. On the right hand side of the main line, the exchange sidings and branch to Wrenthorpe Colliery appear to have been abandoned. *(Aerofilms Ltd.)*

Above: Another view from Westgate North box, this time showing J39 No. 64839 wheeling an Ardsley-bound through freight past Wakefield's Stanier 2-6-4T No. 42650 on 3rd June, 1961. *(Peter Rose)*

WAKEFIELD WESTGATE STATION: Drivers of Up and Down passenger trains calling at Wakefield Westgate must be prepared to stop with the locomotive and leading vehicles beyond the platform end and when the length of the train exceeds six vehicles. The extent to which this is necessary will be indicated to drivers by the station master or other appointed person; it must NOT be taken as authority to pass a stop signal at danger. *Eastern Region(North) Section Appendix, 1968.*

Below: The layout at Westgate in 1914. *(Not to scale)*

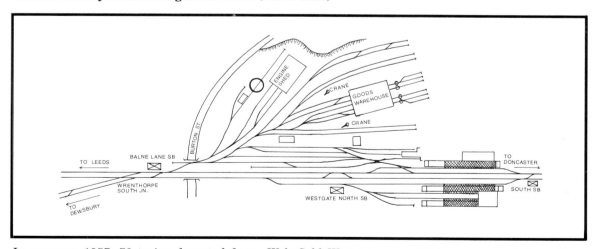

In summer, 1957, 78 trains departed from Wakefield Westgate every 24 hours on weekdays. They included 15 local and 9 express trains to Leeds Central, 9 to Doncaster, 11 to Kings Cross, 17 to Bradford via Dewsbury, 5 express portions to Bradford (one calling at Morley Top), two expresses to Bradford via Leeds and two expresses to Harrogate. Three trains ran to Huddersfield, one each to Castleford Central, Batley via Dewsbury, Cleethorpes, Lincoln Central, and one express to Halifax via Bradford.

Above: Classic West Riding steam in a classic setting. N1 0-6-2T No. 69452 simmers at the north end of Westgate station with the goods warehouse behind on 14th September, 1956. The N1s were prolific performers out of Westgate, especially on the Bradford portions of London expresses. *(P.H.Groom)*

Below: Engine power which looks more appropriate to Kirkgate station rather than the predominantly GN Westgate as seen from Westgate North signal box on 3rd June, 1961. With the goods warehouse in the background, Hughes-Fowler Crab 2-6-0 No. 42863 waits alongside ex-Midland 3F 0-6-0T No. 47255. *(Peter Rose)*

SHORT MEMORIES

January 1961: J94 0-6-0STs 68008/11/5/45 transferred from Copley Hill to Ardsley as replacements for EWYU J52s 68869/75, the last of their class in capital stock

13.5.61: Kentish Town Royal Scot 46160 *Queen Victoria's Rifleman* works a Rugby League cup final special through Wakefield and Pontefract on its way from Leeds Central to St. Pancras.

17.5.61: Bushbury Scot 46167 *The Hertfordshire Regiment* arrives at Healey Mills with a freight from Bescot.

May, 1961: Cardiff Britannias 70022 and 70027 spend four days on Wakefield shed while en-route to Doncaster works.

Three aspects of the old Wakefield Westgate.

Top: Stanier 2-6-4T No. 42649 has arrived with the 12.33pm Bradford to Kings Cross portion on 7th May, 1963. After Wakefield passengers have alighted, the loco in the distance will draw the coaches back into a siding. When the main train arrives from Leeds, the coaches will be attached to the rear. Most Kings Cross trains had Bradford portions then but in 1994 Bradford had just one through train, via Leeds. Portions ceased to be dealt with at Wakefield on 30th April, 1967 when they were switched to Leeds City. *(David Holmes)*

Centre: The exterior of Westgate station, complete with 'classic' cars on 4th August, 1966. These buildings were demolished soon after and the station extensively modernised, work being completed by spring, 1967. *(British Rail)*

Bottom: The Dickensian interior of Westgate South box in December, 1959. *(Tony Ross)*

Above: The south end of Westgate platforms in 1994 look surprisingly unchanged - electrification apart - from this view on 4th September, 1962 in which Class A2/3 Pacific 60523 Sun Castle receives the 'right away' for Kings Cross. *(Peter Rose)*

WAKEFIELD WESTGATE SOUTH SIGNAL BOX: The Down Main or Down Main to platform calling on signals provided at Wakefield Westgate South signal box may be taken off before trains are brought to a stand at them and drivers in such circumstances must draw forward cautiously. *Eastern Region (North) Sectional Appendix, 1968.*

Below: Looking south from the station footbridge on 3rd June, 1961 as B1 4-6-0 No. 61170 prepares to leave with a Doncaster stopping train. *(Peter Rose)*

SHORT MEMORIES

16.9.61: V2 2-6-2s 60861/84 transferred to the former LMS Wakefield shed.

16.9.61: A3s 60036/69/70/77 transferred to Ardsley.

30.9.61: World speed record holding A4 Pacific 60022 *Mallard* travels via Hare Park, Crofton and Calls at Wakefield Kirkgate on its way from Retford to Blackpool with a special train to mark the 90th anniversary of the Northern Rubber Co.

October, 1961: Royal Scots 46117 *Welsh Guardsman* & 46145 *The Duke of Wellington's Regt.* transferred from Low Moor to Mirfield, work a number of freights from Healey Mills to Liverpool. Newport and Crewe.

48

Great Central 2-8-0s at the southern approach to Westgate station.
Above: Class O1 2-8-0 No. 63879, in superb external condition, rolls a train of empties out of
the station on 4th September, 1962. The O1s were Edward Thompson's LNER rebuilds of the
O4s from 1944 with B1-style boilers and Walschaerts valve gear.
Below: Seen from Westgate South signal box doorway on 19th August, 1961, Class O4/ 1 No.
63576 approaches the station with a heavy mixed goods. A Frodingham engine, No. 63576
was one of the original 2-8-0s built for the GC from 1911 onwards to the design of its chief
mechanical engineer, J. G. Robinson. It had the original small boiler, steam and vacuum
brakes and a water scoop. *(Both Peter Rose)*

Above: Sandal, the first station out of Wakefield on the West Riding and Grimsby line to Doncaster, on 24th August, 1957 as an Ivatt Class 4 2-6-0 arrives with a stopping train to Leeds. This passenger station closed on 4th November, 1957 and the goods yard, behind the buildings to the right, on 14th September, 1959. A new station, called Sandal and Agbrigg ,was opened here in November, 1987. *(G.C. Lewthwaite)*

Below: A beautiful shot of Gresley K2 2-6-0 No. 1751 climbing away from Sandal with a southbound freight in late LNER days..The curve to the Midland line at West Riding Junction, closed in 1938, climbs away on the left. *(Ernest Sanderson)*

SHORT MEMORIES

1.1.62: Calder Valley diesel units take over many of the Manchester Victoria-Wakefield Kirkgate - York/Goole services.

7.4.62: A1s 60123/31/4/5 transferred from Copley Hill to Ardsley.

12.9.62: Ex-works Thornaby Class 3 2-6-0 77001 arrives at Healey Milles on a freight from Crewe.

22.8.63: A3 60045 *Lemberg* leaves Healey Mills with a freight to Tyne yard after working the 10.10pm Tyne Yard-Mirfield.
A4 60006 *Sir Ralph Wedgewood* is on the same duty on 13th Sept.

Above: Hare Park Junction was, and stil is, the spot where the former L&Y line from Crofton West joined the West Riding and Grimsby. Class 04/8 2-8-0 No. 63633 brings a southbound coal train past the signal box and onto the main line in spectacular style during 1955. (*Tony Ross.*)

Below: Immediately after the junction came Hare Park and Crofton station. It closed on 4th February, 1952 but was still intact on 21st September, 1958 when D11 4-4-0 No. 62660 *Butler Henderson* paused there with a Down RCTS special. Now preserved by the National Railway Museum, *Butler Henderson* was the first of the GC Large Directors. The buildings on the left were still there in 1994.(*G.C. Lewthwaite*)

Above: Nostell station, closed to passengers on 29th October, 1951 and to goods on 14th September, 1959, was already denuded of its facilities by spring, 1963 when a Peak Type 4 diesel(later Class 46) was passing at full 70mph line speed with a Kings Cross express. The goods yard was still active as exchange sidings for Nostell Colliery and remained so until its rail connection, which went away top right, was closed in the early 1980s.
Nostell signal box is just visible but in later years access to the yard was controlled by a ground frame. Two boys on the site of the Up platforms demonstrate that railway trespass is not a recent problem although their intentions then were probably more innocent than they would be today. *(Roger Hepworth)*
Below: The layout at Nostell in 1914. *(Not to scale)*
The Nostell Colliery railway also served a brick and tile works and a rare feature until the end was a turntable giving access to the engine shed which in the mid-1970s was home to four diesels, one built by the North British Locomotive Co.,one by F.C.Hibberd, one by Yorkshire Engine Co., and one by Rolls Royce.

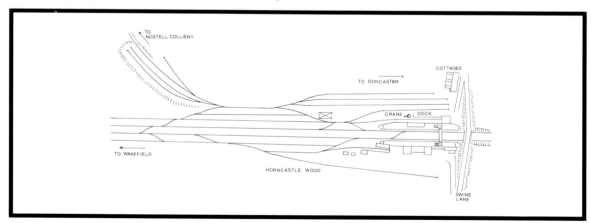

NOSTELL to STAINCROSS(SMITHIES) INCLUDING WHARNCLIFFE WOODMOOR BRANCH: An electric warning gong fixed by the side of the Down line, 164 yards north of the Down Home signal, at a distance of 100 yards from the summit, is for the purpose of warning drivers on the Down line of the incline through Staincross station to Smithies. *NE Region Sectional Appendix, 1960.*

THE EAST & WEST YORKSHIRE UNION

Above: Possibly the biggest engines to regularly work the East and West Yorkshire Union were the J6 0-6-0s. Here, Ardsley's 64226 passes the site of Robin Hood engine shed, closed 1926, while en-route towards Lofthouse Junction on 15th March, 1961. (*Peter Cookson*)

The East and West Yorkshire Union Railway ran just under five miles from Lofthouse North to Stourton. The principal centre on the line was Robin Hood where there was a colliery and coking works, and from where steeply graded branches went west to Thorpe quarries, north to Beeston Colliery, and east to Newmarket Colliery. There was once an engine shed in the triangular junction with the Beeston branch.

There was no block signalling and the whole system was subject to a 15 mph speed limit.

It was worked under 'One Engine in Steam' rules between Robin Hood and Stourton, between Patrick Green and Newmarket Colliery, and along the Thorpe branch which was one mile, 374 yards long.

The 1960 N.E. Region Sectional Appendix included special instructions regarding the EWYU:

"The single line between the Stop Board in the Up siding at Robin Hood and the caution board fixed at the Robin Hood end of the run-round road at Patrick Green is worked......by Train Staff and Ticket. The shunter at Robin Hood will be responsible for the Staff and Ticket working over this section of the line, each of the guards being in possession of a key of the cabin at Patrick Green. When a train runs over this portion of the line from the Robin Hood end, the guard must, if the driver is in possession of the Staff and not requiring to return with it, immediately place the Staff in the rack provided in the Patrick Green cabin; if the driver is in poss-

ession of a Ticket the guard must collect the Ticket at Patrick Green, endorse it 'cancelled' and place it in the box provided in the cabin there. When a train requires to run over this portion of the line from the Patrick Green end, the guard must, if the Staff has been left in the Patrick Green cabin, obtain it from the rack or, if the train is required to be worked with a Ticket, obtain one of the Patrick Green to Robin Hood Tickets from the box in the cabin, which is unlocked by the Train Staff and, having re-locked the Ticket box, show the Staff to the driver, hand him the Ticket and then return the staff to the rack in the cabin.

Patrick Green is the crossing station for trains passing over the single line on each side.

When a train arrives at Lofthouse East and West sidings from Robin Hood it must come to a stand at the Stop Board and await authority of the shunter before any movement is made.

The shunter must ensure that NCB locomotives which may conflict are at a stand before allowing any movement of trains standing at the Stop Board, and that there are no conflicting movements from the North box end of the East and West yard. The shunter must put the signal at that point(controlled by the ground frame) to danger....The locomotive must then be detached and run round the train and after being re-attached at the rear, dispose of its wagons by shunting them off to the various roads, the guard uncoupling them between the Stop Board and the bridge..."

Top: Again, with the site of Robin Hood engine shed on the left, J6 0-6-0s 64222 and 64268 head a southbound Railway Travel and Correspondence Society special at 1pm on 21st September, 1958. *(David Holmes)*

Centre: Robin Hood station with its wooden buildings and signal box, looking towards Stourton on 15th March, 1961. *(Peter Cookson)*

Bottom: In early 1961 a batch of J94 0-6-0STs allocated to Ardsley replaced the GN J52s which previously worked the line.

At 7.30pm on 28th June of that year, No. 68049 rests alongside Robin Hood station. This spot was a regular resting place between jobs which included trips on the steeply graded branches to Newmarket and Beeston collieries and Thorpe Quarries. *(David Holmes)*

Left: J52 0-6-0ST No. 68834 brings a long train of fitted 16-ton mineral wagons into Robin Hood from the Rothwell direction, possibly a special load of coal or coke, at 12.30pm on 14th August, 1959. The line of wagons on the left traces the south-north curve of the Beeston Colliery branch. *(David Holmes)*
Below: Robin Hood in 1921, *(Not to scale)*

BEESTON & THORPE BRANCHES: As there is no block working on these single lines, which are also used by private locomotives when necessary, drivers must keep a sharp lookout and be prepared to stop at any time.

PUBLIC ROAD LEVEL CROSSINGS exist at Wakefield Road, Patrick Green and Milner Lane. A flagman is stationed at Patrick Green and drivers must be prepared to act in accordance with any signal received from the flagman and...the gates will be across the line. Drivers must be prepared to stop clear of this crossing for the gates to be opened by the guard or shunter..."
NE Region Sectional Appendix, 1960.

The Appendix also told guards to pin down the brakes on both sides of all wagons on their trains before starting down the 1 in 30/38 incline from Armitage's sidings, Thorpe, to Robin Hood.

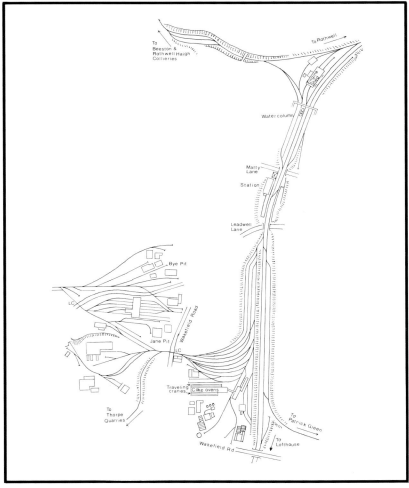

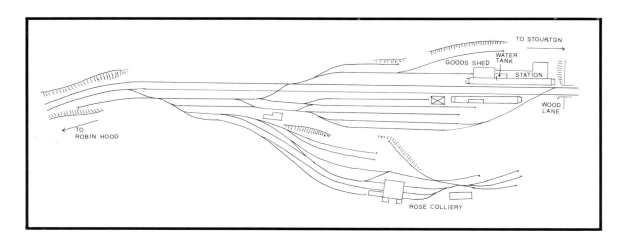

While Robin Hood was the operating centre of the EWYUR, Rothwell was its administrative headquarters.

Top: The layout at Rothwell in 1921. (*Not to scale*)

Centre: Less usual power for an RCTS special on 19th May 1962 in the shape of Ivatt Class 2 2-6-2T No. 41273. The goods shed is on the left while just visible above the train are the station buildings that were once the EWYU headquarters. Only the foundations remained in 1994. (*Arthur Wilson*)

Bottom: One of Mrs. Cotton's excursions receives a rousing send-off as one of the last two J52s, No. 68869, and J6 64222, get the train moving on 21st August, 1961. How sad, though, that the waving children are not going to the sea-

THE LANCASHIRE & YORKSHIRE

Top: A long way from past glories, Britannia Pacific 70004 *William Shakespeare* nears Locke's Siding at the eastern end of the L&Y main line, a quarter of a mile south of Goose Hill Junction, with an east-bound parcels train in August, 1966. No. 70004 was by then based at Stockport which clearly looked after it well. *(Peter Cookson)*

Left: Locke's Siding was the exchange point with the St. John's Colliery complex where steam action could still be savoured into the 1970s. The colliery's Hudswell Clarke 0-6-0T No. S102 *Catheryn* (1884/55) was still at work there on 11th August, 1972. *(David Holmes)*

FREIGHT TRAINS WORKING BETWEEN LOCKE'S SIDING AND NORMANTON. Locomotives and brake vans and cattle trains, from North to South or vice-versa, must as far as practicable, travel over the passenger lines unless the goods lines are clear throughout.

The title of all freight trains from South Yard to Wakefield and beyond must be transmitted to Wakefield East Junction, and the trains must be sent forward along the main line or loop line, according to instructions received from Wakefield East Junction, and the signalman at Wakefield East Junction must obtain his instructions from the joint inspector in the yard. *Eastern Region(North) Sectional Appendix, 1968.*

Originally closer to Kirkgate station, Wakefield motive power depot was rebuilt and expanded around the time of the first world war to cope with increasingly heavy coal traffic produced by the area's many pits.

Under the LMS and early BR it was coded 25A, top of its district with sub-sheds over a wide area from Goole to Sowerby Bridge. In 1957 it was transferred to the N.E. region, becoming 56A with Ardsley under its wing and receiving an influx of ex-LNER locomotives.

Predominantly a freight depot, it did have a few passenger engines, especially in later years although by then the austere WD 2-8-0s made up the bulk of Wakefield's fleet.

Plans to make it a diesel maintenance depot over Healey Mills did not materialise and the shed reamained all steam until closing on 3rd June, 1967. For the next year it was a grim gathering ground for withdrawn engines on their way to scrapyards throughout the North East, before becoming a wagon repair depot until that too closed in 1984. The shed survived until being demolished in spring, 1993.

Below: Many old L&Y types continued to work from Wakefield until the early 1960s. Still active well into the 1950s were the Aspinall 2-4-2Ts, such as 50818, on shed on 17th October, 1956. *(David Holmes)*

Above: The west end of Wakefield shed on 31st December, 1966 with 9F 2-10-0, 8F and WD 2-8-0s and 2-6-4Ts predominating. *(Brian Myland)*

Donald Speight, a former Knottingley train crew supervisor who on 25th April, 1993 had the honour of naming Class 58 58043 *Knottingley*, began his 48-year footplate career at Wakefield shed in 1934, working also at Healey Mills and Normanton.

He recalls: "Wakefield was a very big depot for freight work and there was a big yard at Crofton. All the coal off the Dearne Valley used to go into Crofton and we took it on to Lancashire.

"We worked all the L&Y goods engines. We called the big 0-8-0s 'Lanky Bombers' after the war. Before then L&Y men called them 'Teddy Bears.'

"When I was a boy my father seemed to spend half his time at Liverpool because they took coal there for shipping and then lodged overnight before working back.

"The Dearne Valley was the making of Wakefield shed. There was a shed nearer the station but the new one was created to cope with all the coal through crofton."

Above: In later years a small number of Jubilee 4-6-0s were allocated to Wakefield shed. One of them was No. 45739 *Ulster*, under the coaling plant on 14th June, 1966. *(Brian Myland)*

LOCOMOTIVES ALLOCATED TO WAKEFIELD

Summer 1950

Ivatt Class 2 2-6-2T: 41250/1/2/3/4; 5MT 4-6-0: 45101/204/5/6/9/21/61/339; Ivatt Class 2 2-6-0: 46438/9; 3F 0-6-0T: 47510/72/3/80/2; 8F 2-8-0: 48502/4/6/11/4; 7F 0-8-0: 49625; 2P/3P 2-4-2T: 50650/6/712/5/62/4/788/99/869/73/86/92/8; 2F 0-6-0ST: 51447; Barton-Wright 2F 0-6-0: 52041/3/4; Aspinall 3F 0-6-0: 52120/50/4/86/235/84/305/19/45/51/3/69/86/433/5/521; Hughes 3F 0-6-0: 52561/76; WD 2-8-0: 90124/57/63/87/97/212/37/42/3/249/92/310/29/33/4/7/9/41/2/53/61/2/3/70/9/80/1/96/7/404/12/4/5/7/581/607/15/7/20/4/31/3/5/7/9/43/4/51/2/4/6/67/73/9/82/92/710/9/22/5/9. Total 122.

June, 1961

Stanier 2-6-2T: 40117; Stanier 2-6-4T: 42649/50; Crab 2-6-0: 42861/2/3; 4F 0-6-0: 44097/457; Ivatt Class 2 2-6-0: 46413; Midland 3F 0-6-0T: 47255; LMS 3F 0-6-0T: 47266/379; Aspinall 3F 0-6-0: 52413/61; B1 4-6-0: 61015 *Duiker*/61017 *Buchbuck*/61024 *Addax*/53/1131/1268/96/1385; O4 2-8-0: 63588/857/64/920; J50: 68904/10/33/9/77; WD 2-8-0: 90047/54/6/61/76/89/100/12/6/24/6/35/230/321/26/39/41/2/8/53/63/70/9/80/2/5/96/404/15/7/29/97/543/81/604/7/15/20/5/31/3/5/9/42/51/4/5/6/78/9/707/10. Total 83.

Right: Resting place for Lanky 0-6-0s and men.
No. 52044, one of the Barton-Wright 0-6-0s, introduced in 1887, takes a break on 11th July, 1951. This loco can still be seen on the Keighley and Worth Valley Railway. Behind is the lodging house where visiting enginemen from all over the L&Y system rested between turns. *(Peter Rose)*

Left: One of the slightly more recent and rather more numerous Aspinall 3F 0-6-0s, 52461, was in store by the time it was photographed on 30th August, 1961.
It was the first of ten 'economy' versions built during the first world war, distinguishable by narrower than usual valences. *(Peter Rose)*

Right: Also out of use on the same day was No. 52413, one of those rebuilt with an extended smokebox and Belpaire firebox. *(Peter Rose)*

Right: One of several variations on the Aspinall 2P 2-4-2Ts, No. 10656 still carrying its LMS number, stands on Wakefield shed on 10th July, 1949.
The engine has an extended smokebox, higher coal rails, enlarged cylinder diameter, and is possibly push-pull fitted. *(G.H. Butland)*

Left: Among LNER types allocated to Wakefield were the J50 0-6-0Ts, such as No. 68939, already dumped at the end of the yard, with the power station sidings in the background, on 30th August, 1961. *(Peter Rose)*

Right: During a visit to Wakefield shed on Sunday 1st July, 1951, two LNWR 0-8-0s were found. No. 49394 of Edge Hill and No. 49281, pictured here, of Sutton Oak. *(Peter Rose)*

Above: A general view of the shed yard at Wakefield as seen from a Goole line train on 19th October, 1966.
With Wakefield power station the backdrop are, from left, the original coaling stage and water tank, the mechanised coaling plant, the shed building and the sand hopper with at least six WD 2-8-0s and a B1 4-6-0 present. *(Roy Wood)*

Left: The date is 23rd May, 1967 and there are only a few days to go before Wakefield shed closes altogether. Among the last of its many WD 2-8-0s was 90363 looking run-down but still ready for action.

Even as late as December, 1966, Wakefield still had an allocation of 73 steam locos, including 45 WDs as well as nine 9F 2-10-0s, nine B1s,, Jubilees *Bellerophon* and *Ulster*, seven Class 4 2-6-4Ts and one Ivatt Class 4 2-6-0. *(Brian Myland)*

Right: Nextdoor to Wakefield depot was the single road engine shed at Wakefield power station with the Central Electricity Generating Board's 1958-built Yorkshire Engine Co. diesel No. 2673 inside on 16th April, 1979. (*Adrian J. Booth*)
Below: Heading along the Goole line were the junctions and yards of Crofton.
In 1960 a WD 2-8-0 and west-bound coal train are about to pass under the Midland line after leaving Crofton Hall yard, which is alongside the Dearne Valley Junction line beyond Crofton West signal box. (*Tony Ross*)

Left: Just east of Crofton East Junction was Crofton permanent way depot, closed in 1994.
The main building and two diesel cranes are pictured on 28th May, 1994, shortly after closure.
The yard behind the photographer consisted of several more sidings and was once stacked with panels of track.
During the 1960s, the NE Region civil engineer's department had its own Ruston 4-wheel diesel, No. 85, for shunting here.

Above: Wakefield Kirkgate station originally had an overall roof as seen here on 28th May, 1962 when Frodingham O4/8 2-8-0 No. 63832 was passing through on an eastbound mineral train. *(Peter Rose)*
Below: The sorry picture on 12th May, 1992 hides the fact that the Pontefract line had just reopened to passengers. Quite a few local trains were using the station and some freight still passed through. *(Stephen Chapman)*

13.9.63: Clayton Type 1 diesels D8501/36 temporarily allocated to Ardsley from where they make a series of test runs over the following weeks.

26.9.63: D8501 sets out with 26 loaded mineral wagons from Healey Mills on a run to Low Moor via Heckmondwyke and back via Wortley. It fails at Heckmondwyke.

12.9.64: A1s 60117/30/33/48 transferred from Copley Hill to Ardsley. Jubilees 45602 and 45661 and Standard 4-6-0s 73103/5 go to Wakefield.

WAKEFIELD KIRKGATE: The calling on signals provided at East and West signal boxes below the Up and Down Through and Up and Down Platform starting signal (Outer Home signals for Kirkgate Station box) may be taken off before trains are brought to a stand at them and drivers in such circumstances must draw forward cautiously...*Eastern Region(North) Sectional Appendix, 1968.*

Top: Looking across the north end of Kirkgate station on 3rd June, 1961 as Saltley Crab No. 42846 comes off Wakefield shed to continue its running-in trials from Horwich works. *(Peter Rose)*
From left, are connections into the parcels depot, the Normanton main line, the carriage shed, Wakefield East signal box, the line to Goole and the goods warehouse sidings.

Centre: The Kirkgate layout was substantially reduced in the early 1980s following the end of parcels traffic.
A Leeds-Sheffield DMU formation approaches the station over the newly simplified layout on 30th June, 1982, shortly after demolition of the carriage shed. *(Steve Chapman)*

Bottom: Wakefield East in happier times. A lampman is attending the L&Y lower quadrant signals as Mirfield Fowler 2-6-4T No. 42406 emerges from the carriage depot and passes the lengthy signal box on 30th August, 1961. *(Peter Rose)*

Top: Kirkgate parcels depot was still busy in the early 1970s, in turn keeping the carriage depot in business and requiring such locomotives as BR/Sulzer Class 25 No.7572 to be stabled there between turns. In 1994, the depot was still very much intact and used as a signal engineers depot, some parcels vans still occupying the little-used sidings. *(Missing Link)*

Centre: The magnificent exterior of Kirkgate station on 12th May, 1992.

The buildings owe their survival to Grade 11 listed status and were then occupied by signal engineers and a taxi firm.. *(Stephen Chapman)*

Bottom: The interior of Kirkgate on 29th June, 1933 with ex-L&Y railmotor No. 10616 between turns on the Dearne Valley service to Edlington. *(H. C. Casserley collection)*

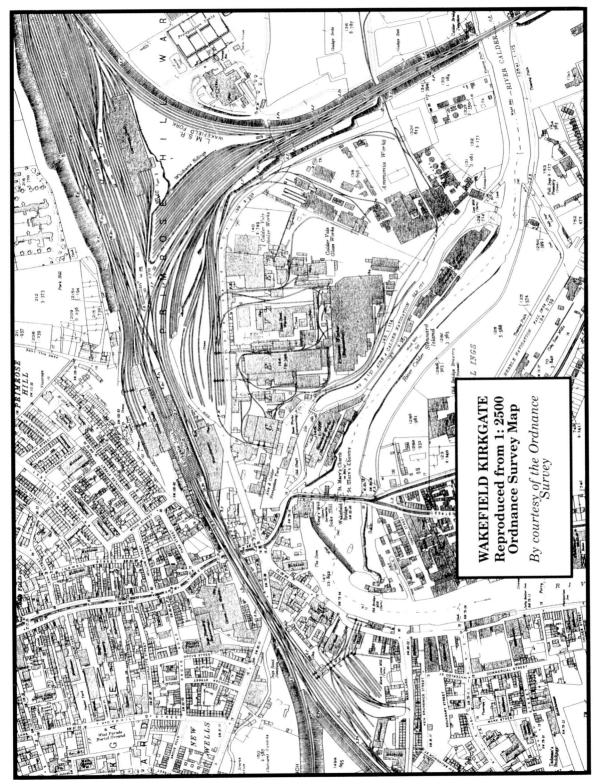

WAKEFIELD KIRKGATE
Reproduced from 1 : 2500
Ordnance Survey Map

By courtesy of the Ordnance Survey

67

Left: A reminder of the time before nationalisation when Wakefield Kirkgate was a joint LMS/LNER station. The water column clearly belonged to the LMS. Below: Space was at a premium at Kirkgate and the Station box was set into the wall, as seen in September, 1962. *(Both Peter Rose)*

In summer, 1957 just over 60 passenger trains called at Wakefield Kirkgate every 24 hours. They included 9 to Normanton, 8 to Barnsley Exchange, 7 to Manchester Victoria, 7 to Goole, 5 to Sowerby Bridge, 3 each to Bradford Exchange, Huddersfield, York, Leeds Central, Wakefield Westgate and Doncaster, 2 to Liverpool Exchange, and one each to Newcastle, Kings Cross, Hull, Blackpool Central and Preston.

By comparison, in winter, 1994 it was served by 108 trains - 33 to Westgate, 27 to Sheffield, 14 to Leeds via Castleford, 14 to Pontefract Monkhill, 9 to Liverpool Lime Street via Huddersfield, 5 to Manchester Victoria via Huddersfield, and three each to Huddersfield and Knottingley.

SHORT MEMORIES

February, 1965: Peak and English Electric Type 4 diesels commence crew training and clearance trials between Healey Mills and Barnsley, Castleford and the Calder Valley.

27.2.1965: Jubilees 45565/45694, B1 61022 and 2-6-4Ts 42161/81 allocated to Wakefield.

23.4.65: Brush Type 4 D1804 arrives at Wakefield depot for crew training and trials in preparation for new merry-go-round workings. Soon after it hauls a 1600-ton train, using slow speed running on the Lofthouse-Methley line.

WAKEFIELD STATION SIGNAL BOX. Drivers of trains on the Up and Down Through and Platform lines entering a section already occupied will be brought nearly to a stand at the Inner Home signal concerned after which the signal will be lowered. Drivers will not be verbally authorised or receive a green hand signal. *Eastern Region (North) Sectional Appendix, 1968.*

Above: On 2nd June, 1961, Crab 2-6-0 No. 42846, running-in after works overhaul, takes its place at the front of Black Five No. 44782 on a York-Liverpool Exchange express . The huge goods warehouse on the right has long since disappeared along with the station roof and L&Y signals.

Below: Again recalling the past importance of Kirkgate, Black Five No. 45338 receives a top-up at the water column during its stop with the 2.2pm York to Liverpool on 2nd August, 1961.
(Both Peter Rose)

Above: Prime motive power for a westbound parcels train on 7th september, 1962 with Carlisle Kingmoor Jubilee 4-6-0 No. 45716 *Swiftsure* in charge.

Below: Three generations of signalling on the south approach to Kirkgate on 2nd June, 1961. Black Five No. 44845 heads Crab 2-6-0 No. 42771 on a York-Liverpool express past electric signals.. In the centre is an L&Y lower quadrant signal while that on the left is pure LMS. Across the background is the three quarter-mile 99-arch viaduct carrying the Leeds-Doncaster line. *(Both Peter Rose)*

Top: In this wonderful scene, Wakefield's Ivatt 2-6-2T No. 41251 has just passed Crigglestone West Junction and is approaching the station with a Barnsley train in 1957. The Wakefield line comes in from the right and the curve from Horbury and Ossett from the left. The distant viaduct carries the Midland line from Royston to Thornhill Junction.

Centre: Looking, south, Fowler 2-6-4T No. 42406 arrives at Crigglestone West with a Barnsley-Wakefield local in 1954. The yard on the left also provided access to the Crigglestone Colliery branch. *(Both Tony Ross)*

Bottom: Following withdrawal by BR, 3F 0-6-0T No. 47445, owned by Hargreaves(West Riding) Ltd. and sporting orange livery, worked on at the sidings serving the British Oak opencast mine.

The sidings were beneath the Midland line viaduct and one of 47445's jobs was to shunt loaded wagons, one at a time, onto staithes for emptying into barges on the Calder and Hebble Navigat ion.

No. 47445 is seen on 5th February , 1967. Rail traffic ended in 1993, the last engine being Hunslet diesel No. 7410. *(Brian Rumary)*

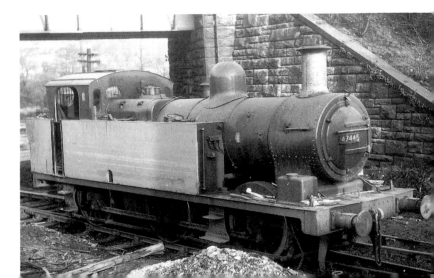

Above: Alien-looking motive power but some ex-NER B16 4-6-0s were allocated to the L&Y shed at Mirfield for working freights from Mirfield and Healey Mills yards. No. 61468 was a B16/3 of the type rebuilt in the 1940s to the design of Edward Thompson.
The station's booking office stands above left of the platform.

Below: Stanier Class 3 2-6-2T No. 40179 calls at the long island platform of Horbury Millfield Road while working the 3.35pm Normanton to Sowerby Bridge on 18th February, 1961. *(Both David Holmes)*

SHORT MEMORIES

August, 1965: The minister of transport approves the closure of Crigglestone and Haigh stations.

January, 1966: English Electric prototype DP2 is a regular visitor to Wakefield Westgate with the 04.00 Kings Cross-Leeds and 10.30 ex-Leeds Yorkshire Pullman.

4.1.66: Jubilee No. 45647 *Sturdee* works a relief to the Up Thames-Clyde through Normanton, which it is believed to have worked through to Leicester.

Spring, 1966: BR proposes to withdraw the Leeds City-Cudworth-Sheffield stopping service from 5th september if there are no objections.

17.4. 66: 75 active steam locos on Wakefield shed.

At Horbury and Ossett the running lines changed from a Down Slow/Down Fast/Up Fast/Up Slow configuration to Down Slow/ Up Slow/ Down Fast/ Up Fast which involved a complex layout

Top: Passing the station on 2nd September, 1961 with the Saturday Only 2.15pm Wakefield to Manchester Victoria are Black Five 45375 and Crab. 42863. The lines from left are Up Slow, Down Fast, Up Fast and Up Loop. *(David Holmes)*

Centre: The track diagramme in Horbury & Ossett box. *(Tony Ross)*

Bottom: The box interior in 1959 with signalman Laurie Mellor and train booker Derek Daley.

A class 2 box with 96 levers, 16 controlling distant signals, Horbury & Ossett was at the end of telephone circuits from Wakefield West and Thornhill No.1, and the booker would relay the descriptions of passing trains to the other boxes on the circuit.

The booker rang a call code on the circuit bell, usually 2-1, and every signalman at each intermediate box would grab the phone and listen to the booker announcing which train was passing. Horbury & Ossett received similar information from the two boxes at the other ends of the circuit.

Its position on the circuit meant that it had 7 telephone circuit bells besides 6 block bells so it could be quite noisy.

This system gave signalmen early warning of approaching trains, allowing them to make effective decisions on train regulation in plenty of time, so keeping traffic moving over a very busy stretch of railway. (*Tony Ross*)

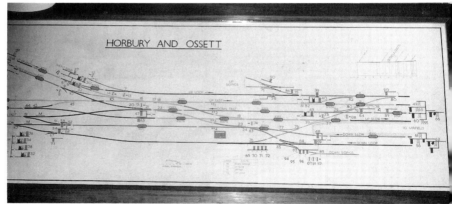

HORBURY AND OSSETT

Above: Between Horbury and Ossett and Healey Mills on a Sunday afternoon in early 1963. A Hunslet 0-6-0 diesel shunter from Wakefield shed and a B1 4-6-0 occupy the siding. The goods depot is in the right distance and the Yorkshire Wagon Works(later Wagon repairs) on the left.

Below: On the same day, a Black Five 4-6-0 heads west with a stopping train to Manchester Victoria. Such trains still pass ed this way in 1994 but they were formed of Pacer diesel rail-buses and travelled via Huddersfield. *(Both Roger Hepworth)*

The many fitted and partly fitted freights passing through Horbury and Ossett at night in 1959/60 included the 8.35pm Manchester Oldham Road-York, 8.35 pm Manchester Victoria-Normanton parcels, the Goole-Aintree Class D, Aintree-Hull Class E, the Holyhead-York cattle. Freights left Healey Mills for Bolton, Stoke, Edge Hill, Bamber Bridge, Manchester Brewery Sidings, Patrifcroft, Brindle Heath, Warring -ton Arpley, Crewe, Bescot, Dewsnap and Holyhead.

The early hours saw many parcels and news-paper trains distributing northern editions printed in Manchester, such as the 12.12 Manchester Exchange-Newcastle, and there was the 1.9am Mirfield-Normanton milk, a portion off the Congleton-Leeds parcels. Other trains included the York-Walton Class C, worked throughout to Liverpool by a York B1.

Above: Recent memories of the Shell oil trains from Stanlow hauled by the dedicated fleet of Class 47s, some named after Shell's ocean-going tankers. No. 47119 *Arcidae* heads the 6M19 Jarrow-Stanlow empties past Horbury and Ossett on 9th September, 1988. The wagon works on the left had by this time gone and occupied the goods yard on the right. *(Stephen Chapman)*

Below: York B16/3 4-6-0 No. 61464 leaves the old Healey Mills yard on 28th October, 1961 with a Class F fitted goods to Stockton-on-Tees.. *(David Holmes)*

Above: The old Healey Mills yard looking west with the main running lines on the left. They are, from left, Up Goods Loops, Up Fast, Down Fast, Up Slow, Down Slow. The signals in the Up direction are Healey Mills East starters, with Healey Mills West inner distants below. In the Down direction they are the Healey Mills Down Homes with Horbury and Ossett distants below. The line between Horbury and Mirfield was so intensely operated and signal boxes so close together that block sections overlapped.

Below: The old Healey Mills looking east from the west end with a Stanier 2-6-0 entering the reception sidings with a freight from across the Pennines. *(Both Tony Ross)*

The 50 year-old marshalling yard at healey Mills was enlarged and modernised in the early 1960s at a cost of £3.75 million, making it one of just three big principal yards in BR's NE Region.

Opened in 1963, it replaced 13 other West Riding yards, including Horbury Junction, Wakefield Exchange, Turner's Lane, New Withams and Crofton Laden sidings.

Before modernisation, Healey Mills consisted of 3 reception and 31 sorting sidings capable of holding a total of 1,572 wagons.

The new complex, over two miles long, had 14 reception sidings with engine line in the middle. The first 7 were for Down traffic, Up Receptions 8 and 9 could only be accessed by reversing from the West End Neck. Up Receptions 10 to 14 were for traffic via the Up Arrival line which left the Up mains at Horbury and climbed over the Up Departure lines to reach the receptions. Up trains could be reversed on to any reception from the West End Neck which was also the way trains from the Royston line reached the yard.

The 50 primary sorting sidings were bordered by 5 staging roads and the diesel depot on the Down side and the flyover line on the Up side. The first 19 roads in the main yard comprised the Down yard, siding 10 being for Down secondary sorts and siding 20 for brake vans. Sidings 21 to 50 formed the Up yard, sidings 49 and 50 being for Up secondary sorts.

Across the yard from the Down side were 7 Down Departure roads, Down engine arrival line, 11 Down secondary roads, Up engine arrival line, 9 Up departure roads, 9 Up staging roads and 19 Up secondary sorting sidings.

The River Calder had to be diverted for the new yard, as did the main lines, the Down passing to the north of the complex and the Up to the south.

A control tower situated just west of the old Healey Mills West signal box controlled most operations in the yard and incorporated a power signal box which initially replaced all manual boxes between Horbury Millfield Road and Thornhill No.1.

The wagonload traffic for which the big yards were intended was already declining and Healey Mills probably never reached its design capacity of 4,000 wagons a day, despite seeing over 70 booked westbound and 50 eastbound departures every 24 hours in June, 1965, plus many other trains which passed through or called for re-manning.

Since the late 1970s, considerable rationalisation has taken place, the hump and reception sidings being completely abandoned. With general freight - latterly Speedlink - and the make-up of coal trains transferred to Doncaster in the late 1980s, leaving only departmental traffic, the future looked bleak.

But in the early 1990s it made a modest comeback which saw part of its accompanying diesel depot reopened after nearly 10 years in mothballs for refuelling and inspection of locomotives used on cross-Pennine oil trains.

Against all the odds, in 1994 the shrunken Healey Mills seemed to have hung on where some other big yards have died altogether.

Below: Early 1963 and work is under way on building the new Healey Mills yard. The view is looking west and new earthworks are taking shape on the south side(left) of the running lines. The Up running lines were diverted in this direction and the new sidings laid out in the centre. (*Roger Hepworth*)

Healey Mills diesel depot, situated on the north side of the marshalling yard and immediately south of the eastbound running lines, was opened in March, 1966 to provide servicing and maintenance facilities for 55 locomotives.

It consisted of a double-ended servicing shed built of a steel frame with asbestos cladding, the lower parts and end walls being brick. Inside were two 70ft inspection pits, a fuelling point, an oil store and office.

The maintenance shed was of similar construction but with insulated asbestos cement cladding, 3 through roads, each with a 140ft pit, and one dead-end road with a 60ft pit. Equipment included four 20-ton electric jacks for bogie cleaning, a 3cwt crane over one through track for removing cylinder heads and other engine parts, battery chargers, stores, and a machine area with lathe and drilling machine. An automatic washer was situated at the west end of the depot.

Three new signalling blocks were added to Healey Mills signal box interlocking for controlling movements on and off the depot.

Some of the first locomotives to be allocated there were English Electric Type 4s D250/4/8/9/75 /82/347/9/50/1/2/3/4/5/85/7/8/97/8, and 350hp 0-6-0 shunters D3071/ 230/1/76/81/97/456/7/873.

A 45-ton steam breakdown crane, No. 330107, was stationed at Healey Mills, from 1967/8. It provided cover in an area bounded by Hebden Bridge, Low Moor, Marsden, Penistone, Barnsley Exchange, Pontefract and Goose Hill Junction. The depot also had two independant snow ploughs.

Initially given the temporary depot code of HM, it was allocated 55C in March, 1968, only to revert to HM when the present computerised system was introduced in the 1970s.

The depot was downgraded to a servicing point, losing its main line allocation, on 1st October, 1984, closing altogether shortly after.

In March, 1993, the servicing shed was reopened, mainly as a fuel and inspection point for locomotives on cross-Pennine freight trains, and in 1994 a good selection of locomotives could still be found 'on shed 'there.

Above: A general view across Healey Mills yard, looking west, on 5th January, 1982 when there was still a good mixture of general freight and coal traffic. *(Peter Rose)*
The English Electric Class 40 diesels, regular performers from Healey Mills since the mid-1960s, had only another year or two left in service.
The Up main lines are on the extreme left and the Down lines on the right.

Tom Hicks was an engineman at Royston shed until November, 1967 when it closed with the end West Riding steam and he, along with many of his workmates, transferred to Healey Mills.

When he arrived there, the first thing he noticed was all the different types of men from different backgrounds - some, like himself, from the Midland, others from the L&Y and others from the GN. They now expected to work over a much greater variety of routes.

"We spent a month road-learning to York, Doncaster and to Middlewich, Cheshire.

"It was a demanding time but the men were a friendly lot and everyone helped each other.

"Turns we had never worked before included the news vans to Manchester Victoria, a very fast train.

"From Healey Mills we worked to Manchester, Agecroft, Newcastle-Trafford Park Freightliners to Manchester and York, oil trains to Toton and local coal trains. We had no passenger work although the spare link did get some Blackpool runs in the summer."

Below: A busy scene at Healey Mills on 5th January, 1982. Class 37s 37131 and 37110 await a relief crew for their eastbound tank train. Other locos from left are Class 31 No. 31107 and Class 47 No. 47308 outside the diesel maintenance shed, 40092 on more eastbound tanks and Class 56 No. 56046 with empty MGR wagons.

NORMANTON & THE MIDLAND

Above: The North Midland from Leeds to Sheffield was still an important part of the Midland route from London to Scotland when Jubilee No. 45597 *Barbados* was photographed racing a northbound express over Oakenshaw South Junction in 1960. *(Tony Ross)*
The battery of signals on the gantry included those controlling the Up Goods and Main lines, plus distants for West Riding Junction and, in the middle, those controlling the Up Goods to Main crossover. In the background are Down distants for Oakenshaw North and signals controlling access to the curve down to the L&Y.
Oakenshaw South and West Riding Junction signal boxes both closed in September, 1965, Oakenshaw North being reframed to handle the longer section. Oakenshaw South Junction was remodelled and the curve singled in February, 1989.
Below: Stanier 2-6-2T 40181 calls at Walton with the Saturday 2.6pm Cudworth to Leeds City on 11th March, 1961. Called Sandal and Walton until 30th September 1951, this station replaced Oakenshaw in 1870, and closed to passengers on 12th June, 1961. (*David Holmes)*

Above: Grimy Black Five No. 44826 hardly seems worthy power for one of the Midland's premier expresses, the Edinburgh to St. Pancras Waverley, as it passes beneath the gantry at Goose Hill in 1960.

The signals are, from left: Up Wakefield Goods home, Up main to Up Wakefield and distant for Locke's Siding, Up main, Up main to Up Goods and distant for St. John's Colliery, next box along the Midland until it closed in 1963. Towering above the whole scene are the chimneys of St. John's brickworks.

Below: The well-polished interior of Goose Hill signal box in 1960. *(Both Tony Ross)*

SHORT MEMORIES

18.6.66: Q6 0-8-0s 63344/87/420/6 transferred to Normanton following closure of Neville Hill to steam.

4.7.66: Ardsley-Laisterdyke line closed to passenger traffic. Its remaining train, the Bradford portion of the 10.20 from Kings Cross, is diverted via the Wortley curve.

27.8.66: Britannia 70021 *Morning Star* passes Kirkgate and Normanton with a Shrewsbury-Newcastle cadet special.

Above: Jubilee No. 45568 *Western Australia* has a good head of steam as it leaves Goose Hill Junction behind while working the 12.25 Leeds to St. Pancras on 24th April, 1962. The L&Y lines from Wakefield are on the left.

Goose Hill box closed in October, 1988 and by September, 1994, only the bottom half remained.

Below: Crab 2-6-0 No. 42938 pulls a southbound unfitted express goods through Normanton station on 2nd May, 1964. *(Both Roy Wood)*

SHORT MEMORIES

Summer, 1966: Normanton enjoys an increase in traffic including more diesel work. Normanton men rostered to work Toton to Normanton freights hauled by Class 47s, which they are not passed on so they have a conductor. Wakefield men work the south-bound trains

October, 1966: Wakefield still has regular work for 75 steam locos. 61 of total allocation are WD 2-8-0s, 12 are B1 4-6-0s.

Being at the southern end of the York and North Midland, one of the constituents of the North Eastern Railway, meant that Normanton saw a good deal of NE motive power on trains from York.

Above: York-based B1 4-6-0 No. 61018 *Gnu* is unusual power for a York-Manchester Victoria express at Normanton Station South on 22nd March, 1961.

Below: Another B1, No. 61053, plods steadily through the station with an Up unfitted express goods on 11th August, 1961 as Stanier 2-6-2T No. 40082 waits in one of the bay platforms with a stopping passenger train, probably to Sowerby Bridge. *(Both Peter Rose)*

Top: Normanton men were familiar with a number of NE types and for a time even had an allocation of Q6 0-8-0s.

Here, No. 63449 was busy on local trip work in the yards alongside the station on 8th June, 1962. *(Roy Wood)*

Centre: The virtual end of steam at Normanton with 8F 2-8-0 No. 48507 standing by Normanton No. 2 Goods signal box on 21st October, 1967.

Bottom: The diesels move in. On the same day, Class 37 No. D6866 stands beneath the station buildings and footbridge with a southbound train of 100-ton oil tanks. *(Both Adrian J. Booth)*

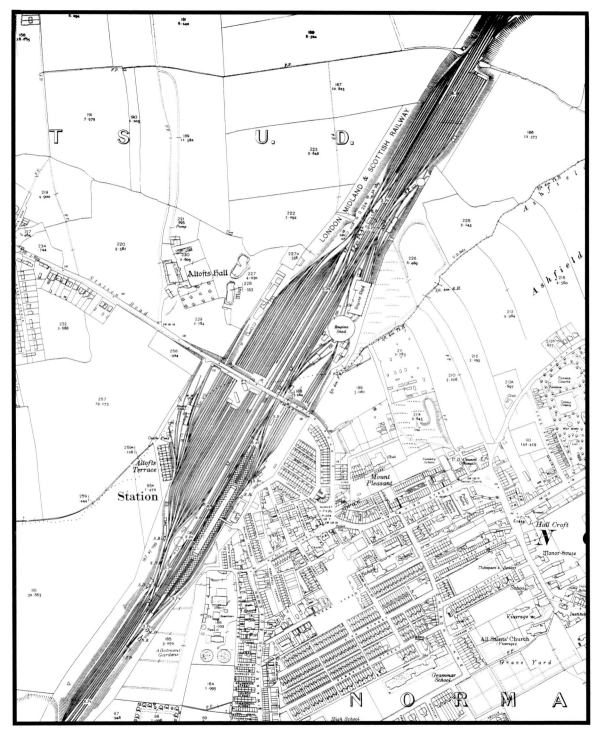

Normanton in 1933 as reproduced from a 1:2500 Ordnance Survey map. It is interesting to note that the motive power depot included a roundhouse at that time. *(By courtesy of the Ordnance Survey)*

Above: On 13th May, 1962 the RCTS ran a railtour from Nottingham Victoria to Darlington hauled by SR Schools class 4-4-0 No. 30925 *Cheltenham* and 3P 4-4-0 No. 40646. The special is seen pausing beneath the imposing if not very pretty Normanton buildings, all of which had been cleared by 1994 along with the track in the foreground. *(Brian Myland)*
Below: Looking north from Normanton's Down platform as Q6 0-8-0 No. 63426 comes to a stand with a coal train from the Castleford direction at 3pm on 4th April, 1966. *(David Holmes)*

Above: Fairburn 2-6-4T No. 42083 holds a fish van in one of the north end bay platforms on 27th June, 1962 while Black Five No. 45018 calls at platform one with a Down express. After being scaled down in the last century, Normanton continued as a significant interchange for parcels and mails until the 1960s, its island platform enabling easy transfers between trains. Below: Royston Crab 2-6-0 No. 42762 is running light through Normanton on 29th August, 1962. *(Both Peter Rose)*

SHORT MEMORIES

Above: Ivatt Class 4 2-6-0 No. 43114 trundles a long trip freight past the locomotive depot and Normanton Station North signal box on 29th August, 1962.

Below: Saltley Black Five No. 45265 pulls its Birmingham - Bradford express away from Normanton on 22nd March, 1961. *(Both Peter Rose)*

8.11.66: Diesels D8068 and D6788 with 4 brake tenders run trial MGR trains from the Snydale branch to Ferrybridge power station.

December, 1966: Wakefield Jubilees 45694 *Bellerophon* and 45739 *Ulster* work Christmas parcels trains to the Calder Valley.

27.12.66: 45694 brings the 09.00 Bradford portion for Kings Cross into Wakefield Westgate and returns to Leeds with the 11.00 departure, a train from Kings Cross.

On weekdays in summer, 1957 there were 57 advertised passenger train departures from Normanton station every 24 hours. They consisted of 10 trains to Leeds City, including both express and stopping trains, nine to Sheffield Midland, eight to Manchester Victoria, six to Bradford Forster Square, five to Sowerby Bridge, four to York, three to St. Pancras, two to Cudworth and one each to Wakefield Kirkgate, Liverpool Exchange, Newcastle, Derby, Bristol, Scarborough and Blackpool Central. In addition, there was a school train to Royston and Notton at 4.15pm, and Friday night holiday trains to Bournemouth West and Paignton. Of the named expresses, only the northbound Devonian stopped at Normanton, at 6.6pm.

Coded 20E under the London Midland Region Leeds district, Normanton became 55E in 1957 when the whole district was transferred to the North Eastern Region.
Towards the end of steam, steam locomotives visiting the West Riding were serviced there following the closure to steam of other sheds like Holbeck and Wakefield. Normanton lost its own steam allocation on 2nd October, 1967, but continued to service visiting LMR steam locomotives and remained a diesel stabling point for a little while longer. Withdrawn steam engines were stored there until May, 1968.
Above: BR Standard Class 5 4-6-0 No. 73160 rests outside its home shed on 29th August, 1962
(Peter Rose)

LOCOMOTIVES ALLOCATED TO NORMANTON

Summer, 1950

Stanier 3 2-6-2T: 40179; Johnson MR 2P 4-4-0: 40406/80, Fowler 2P 4-4-0: 40630; Johnson 1F 0-6-0T: 41793/844; Johnson 3F 0-6-0: 43301/497/509/14/639/56/714; 4F 0-6-0: 44098/9/ 151/217/336/7/8/562/86/603/4; Johnson 3F 0-6-0T: 47239; LMS 3F 0-6-0T: 47334/5/405; 8F 2-8-0: 48084/130/1/46/60/4/266/71/4/352/7/94/5/6/507/8/670/702; Aspinall 2-4-2T: 50621; Aspinall 3F 0-6-0: 52089. Total: 49.

November, 1966

4MT 2-6-4T: 42083/149; Ivatt 4MT 2-6-0: 43043/98/125/9; WD 2-8-0: 90054/243/ 337/465 / 503/ 617/44/82/99/721/2; Drewery 204hp 0-6-0 diesel: D2262/323/4; BR 350hp 0-6-0 diesel: D3876. Total 21.

LOCOMOTIVES ON NORMANTON SHED: 9TH NOVEMBER, 1952

Stanier Class 3 2-6-2T: 40075/179; Johnson 2P 4-4-0: 40480; LMS 2P 4-4-0: 40630; 1F 0-6-0T: 41661/844; Fairburn 2-6-4T: 42141; 3F 0-6-0: 43509/639/56/714/832; Midland 4F 0-6-0: 43852/4010; LMS 4F 0-6-0: 44098/9/151/217/337/514/586/603/4; Midland 3F 0-6-0T: 47239; LMS 3F 0-6-0T: 47334/5/405; Beyer-Garratt 2-6-6-2: 47990; 8F 2-8-0:48069/76/84/146/60/202/ 66/74/352/57/96/7/ 670/6/702; WD 2-8-0: 90231/487/675; Aspinall 3F 0-6-0: 52089; J71 0-6-0T: 68238/92/4. Total: 52.

SHORT MEMORIES

November, 1966: Many Wakefield area freight workings are dieselised and MGR operation becomes more commonplace, but 75% of Goole line freight is still steam, usually Black Five or B1 4-6-0s, 8F and WD 2-8-0s and 9F 2-10-0s.

January, 1967: Holbeck Jubilee 45675 *Hardy* is reduced to working coal trains on the Wakefield-Goole line.

2.1.67: The Wakefield-Goole passenger service is withdrawn A new Leeds-Goole service via Methley is introduced.

4F 0-6-0 No. 44336, Crab 2-6-0 No. 42702 and WD 2-8-0 No. 90254 resident inside Normanton shed on 29th August, 1962 (above) while making a fine portrait outside(below) was Fairburn 2-6-4T No. 42149. (*Peter Rose*)

SHORT MEMORIES

January, 1967: Healey Mills receives 13 Class 37 diesels from the Western region for Calder Valley freight work.

25.2.67: Class 11 diesel shunter No. 12113 is allocated to Normanton.

18.3.67: Because a Dutch vessel is stuck in mud beneath Selby swing bridge, a returning Britannia-hauled Barrow-Hull soccer special is diverted via Wakefield and Goole.

18.5.67: Black Five 44767 hauls four withdrawn steam locos through Kirkgate to Hull via Goole for scrap. It returns light later that day.

July 1967: 3 2-6-4Ts, 5 Black Fives, 7 WDs and an Ivatt 4 2-6-0 transferred to Normanton.

Above: Stanier 2-6-2T N0. 40181 from Royston was stored at the south end of Normanton shed yard on 27th June, 1962. The shed andwater tank are in the background with the site of the roundhouse just behind the locos.
Below: Holbeck Caprotti Black Five 44754 was alongside the coaling plant on 22nd March, 1961 as Darlington B1 61304 was taking water. (*Both Peter Rose*)

Above: Normanton MPD in July, 1967 with both coal and ash plants visible. Locomotives present include WD 2-8-0s 90722 and 90644, a pair of Ivatt 4MT 2-6-0s and, on the left, a BR/Sulzer Class 25 diesel. *(Peter Rose)*

Below: Steam depots were in reality filthy and inhospitable places to work in, especially towards the end of steam, as this view of Normanton ash plant illustrates. In company with narrow gauge wagons used for removing ash from the pit, were LMR Black Fives 44894 and 44816. The date is 4th November, 1967, the last day of West Riding steam. *(Adrian J. Booth)*

Normanton tanks.
Right: A small stud of ex-NER 0-6-0Ts was kept at Normanton for shunting the Castleford goods branch..
On 11th July, 1948 Class J71 No. 8298(still in LNER livery) was on shed with ex-Mildand 4F 0-6-0 No. 3913.
(G.H. Butland)

By the time this picture was taken on 22nd March, 1961, the J71s had given way to J72s such as No.68726. *(Peter Rose)*

The Johnson 1F 0-6-0Ts were among indigenous shunting engines based at Normanton. LMS No. 1844 was present on shed on 11th July, 1948.
(G.H.Butland)

Above: The LMS Beyer-Garratts regulary powered heavy mineral trains from the East Midlands to York. Sometimes they made it on to Normanton shed, where 47984 was photographed on 11th July, 1948. *(G.H.Butland)*

Below: B1 4-6-0 No. 61304 has just taken water while Midland 4F 0-6-0 No. 43968 waits in the queue. *(Peter Rose)*

SHORT MEMORIES

September, 1967:: Normanton crews learn BR/ Sulzer Type 2 diesels.

4.11.67: 8F 48276 of Royston works the 15.00 Carlton-Goole freight, the last steam turn for a West Riding locomotive.

6.11.67: One of four last steam passenger trains is the 17.47 FO Manchester Exchange-York. The engine, usually a Britannia, stables at Normanton before working the 03.10 MO Normanton-Halifax.

6.11.67: Leeds-Doncaster local service withdrawn.

4.12.67: Britannia 70014 *Iron Duke* brings a train of mineral empties from Middleton Junction into Healey

SHORT MEMORIES

June, 1968: Steam freights still reaching Healey Mills are 22.16 Bolton-Hull. 03.25 return from Hull; 07.30 from Middleton Jn., 12.15 to Brewery Sidings; 10.45 from Wyre Dock; 13.02 from Stalybridge; 14.30 from Bolton and 18.10 to Middleton Jn. Most 8Fs with some Black Fives.

11.8.68: Britannia 70013 *Oliver Cromwell,* man-ned by Healey Mills men, passes through Kirkgate en-route to Bressingham for preservation after working the last BR steam train.

October, 1968: Peckett 0-4-0ST No. 2020/42 working at British Oak

Above: The wooden Altofts and Whitwood halt as it was, still with gas lamps, on 8th July, 1967.
Later known simply as Altofts, the station closed in 1990 but was still in situ, minus buildings and fittings, on the freight only Altofts-Methley section, in September, 1994. *(G.C. Lewthwaite)*

Below: Holbeck Jubilee 4-6-0 No. 45562 *Alberta* coasts a six-coach Leeds City to Sheffield Midland stopping train round the long, sweeping curve from Methley to Altofts Junction in the 1960s. *(Peter Cookson)*

Above: With the Methley Joint line passing over the top, Stanier 2-6-2T 40181 rounds the curve towards Methley Junction with the 2.9pm Cudworth -Leeds on 23rd September, 1961..
Below: A third colliery still using steam in the 1970s was Savile Colliery at the end of a short branch from Methley North.
NCB North Yorkshire Area Hunslet 0-6-0ST No. S111 *Airedale No. 2* was shunting side tippler wagons full of dirt alongside the River Aire on 10th May, 1972. *(Both David Holmes)*
By 1975, S111 was out of use and one Hunslet and two Hudswell Clarke diesels were in charge. The connection to BR was closed on 23rd February, 1981 but the internal rail system continued to be used for moving spoil and loading barges until the pit closed in September,